The Seven Mountain Mandate

Taking Your Place of Influence

Endorsements

This book is a prophetic trumpet blast for our time. In an hour when revival is stirring across college campuses and throughout the nation, Laurie Skipper reminds us that revival must lead to awakening and awakening to true reformation. With biblical depth and practical clarity, she unpacks the Seven Mountain Mandate and calls believers to rise with Kingdom authority, reclaim influence, and disciple nations. It is a roadmap and a rallying cry for all who long to see cultural transformation and the fulfillment of Christ's command that the kingdoms of this world become the Kingdom of our Lord.

What sets *The Seven Mountain Mandate: Taking Your Place of Influence* apart is its unwavering call to action. It does not stop at inspiration but equips readers with a clear vision of their role in advancing the Kingdom in every sphere of culture. It compels us to move beyond passivity, to recognize our place in God's design, and to engage society with boldness, wisdom, and righteousness. This is more than a message, it is a divine strategy to see lives, cities, and nations transformed for generations to come.

Dr. Scott Reece
Lead Pastor, River City Church
Executive Director, The Azusa Network

******

In *The Seven Mountain Mandate: Taking Your Place of Influence*, Laurie Skipper has produced a powerful and strategic work that carries both clarity and prophetic urgency for this hour. Having pioneered an apostolic network in the US and ministered globally for decades, I recognize the importance of clear teaching that not only defines the mountains of cultural influence but also equips the Body of Christ to occupy them with Kingdom authority. Laurie's writing provides a comprehensive history of this message while breaking fresh ground by showing how the five-fold ministry intersects with every sphere of society. This integration is vital for advancing true Kingdom transformation.

This message is a trumpet call to believers everywhere to rise up and take their place of influence. Laurie reminds us that revival must lead to reformation and that nations are discipled when God's sons and daughters bring His Kingdom into every arena of culture. I wholeheartedly endorse this work and believe it will serve as a key resource to equip leaders who are serious about advancing God's purposes in cities and nations.

Barbara Wentroble
Founder & President, International Breakthrough Ministries
Author of *Courageous Women Leaders* and other books

******

This book is more than teaching – it is a trumpet call. The Seven Mountain Mandate reveals that revival must mature into reformation if we are to see nations transformed and cultures reclaimed for the Kingdom of God. Every believer who desires to shape history rather than watch it unfold must read and respond to this message.

Jane Hamon, Christian International
Author of *Discernment*, *Dreams and Visions*, *Confronting the Thief*, *The Deborah Company*, *Declarations for Breakthrough*, and *The Cyrus Decree*

Laurie Skipper has given the body of Christ a timely, clarifying, and empowering resource. With clarity and conviction, she not only traces the history of the Seven Mountain Mandate but also equips believers with the practical tools we need to engage culture with Kingdom influence. What I appreciate most is how she weaves together biblical foundation, historical insight, and practical application – bringing both revelation and a roadmap. This is not just theory; it is a call to action for every believer who longs to see revival lead to true transformation. If you want to understand your assignment in this critical hour and step into your God-given sphere of influence with boldness and wisdom, this book is for you.

Dr. Brent Simpson, Lead Pastor, Arise Church
Overseer, Arise Global Network
Author of *The Man's Manifest: Rediscovering the Man Within the Male* and *Where's the Beef: Reclaiming the Power of God in Your Life and Ministry*

******

Laurie Skipper's new book, *The Seven Mountain Mandate: Taking Your Place of Influence*, is both fascinating and enlightening. She unveils key insights regarding the Seven Mountains of cultural influence. Presented with both clarity and depth, her style and voice also add a distinctive, prophetic edge that is powerfully engaging, offering both historical context and present-day application. Read and discover; Laurie Skipper has put together a well written, and well-documented resource that will not only open your eyes and stir your heart but will equip you to take your God-given "place of influence" on the mountain(s) to which you are assigned.

Dr. Tommy Pierce
John17Ministries
Adjunct Professor, Kingdom University

******

The work that Laurie has done in researching roots and outworkings of the Seven Mountains message is very impressive. This book is key in taking one's understanding beyond just the cliches of the mandate. The deeper dive she has done with accompanying testimonies is quite exciting and, I think, ultimately catalytic. I highly recommend this book, and well done, Laurie!

Johnny Enlow, Restore Seven
Author of *Seven Mountain Prophecy*, *The Seven Mountain Mantle*, *RISE: A Reformer's Handbook for the Seven Mountains*, and other books

******

Laurie Skipper has authored a book that is both deeply researched and clearly personal. The Seven Mountain Mandate is not just a study; it is a call. Every page reveals the wisdom and spiritual insight she has gained from faithfully studying the Word of God. Laurie challenges readers to recognize their unique area of influence and equips them with practical ways to step into who they are called to be and where they are called to serve the Lord. She honors God in every word and points clearly to Him as the source of purpose for which so many are searching. This is a solid and inspiring guide for anyone who desires to live with greater clarity and impact.

Tina Blount
Ministry Development Pastor & Leader of Arise Entrepreneurs, Arise Church
Author of *Your Life is a Tree of Possibilities: Discover how to express your purpose and bear fruit in every season of life*, *Warnings to the Seven Churches: Parasites in the Body of Christ*, and *Now What?: Finding Life Through A Layoff...and a Job Too!*

******

I first met Laurie Skipper in the early 1990s while she was a student at the Bible college where I served. I witnessed firsthand her love for God, her devotion to biblical truth, and her commitment to scholarship as I monitored her progress. Over the years we stayed in touch, and I have seen her faithfully live out her calling through a lengthy career in the marketplace and significant involvement in church ministry.

As God led me into ministry in Latin America as a representative of Christian International Global Network, I became increasingly aware of the need for the Body of Christ to understand the "seven mountain mandate," to be salt and light in our sphere of influence, and to disciple nations so that revival and societal transformation can come, fulfilling the prayer Jesus taught us: "Thy Kingdom come, Thy will be done on earth as it is in Heaven." Jesus would not have instructed us to pray this way if the answer were not possible.

Yet many believers, though passionate, lacked the wisdom, strategies, and practical guidelines needed to move from conviction to implementation. That is why *The Seven Mountain Mandate: Taking Your Place of Influence* is such a timely and important book. Laurie Skipper not only unpacks the biblical foundations and spiritual dynamics of the seven mountain mandate, but she also provides real-life examples, practical tools, and workable strategies that enable readers to step confidently into their place of influence.

This book is both deeply insightful and highly practical. It is powerful resource that informs the mind, stirs the spirit, and equips believers to see lasting results rather than repeated frustrations. I highly recommend it.

Prophet Cliff Bell
Representative in Latin America, Christian International Global Network

******

Laurie Skipper has been considered a cherished member of our family by three generations of ministers. Our family has watched her grow from the young child who accepted Christ to the prophet she is today. Her life exemplifies the principles of following Christ and pursuing His calling. As a gifted teacher of the Word, she shares profound knowledge of the kingdom of God. One area in which she is particularly used is to activate the gifts of the Holy Spirit within individuals.

In this book, Laurie explains each of the seven mountains in detail and guides readers in identifying their mountain. She explains the process of moving from recognizing our mountain to taking actionable steps within our sphere of influence to take our mountain for God's kingdom. These steps encourage us to come together with others who are in our sphere of influence and claim our territory. Additionally, she weaves in the role of the five-fold ministry with respect to bringing kingdom influence to the Seven Mountains, providing clarity in that calling, and a structured framework for achieving your assignment within the body of Christ.

May the revelation and wisdom in this book awaken and equip you to fulfill your destiny in this now season.

Paul and Evelyn Williams, Pastors
Audra Williams Smith, Co-Pastor
Orlando International Worship Center

Reading this book stirred something deep within me. As I have been growing in my understanding of what the Kingdom of God truly means, I am reminded that our identity as sons and daughters of God is inseparable from our assignment in the earth as part of both the

Ekklesia and Oikos. Jesus made it so clear when He sent out the seventy (in Luke 10) and then the twelve (in Matthew 10 and Mark 6) that their message was about declaring, "The Kingdom is at hand." That reality was there then – and it still is today.

After the finished work of the cross, that same Kingdom message was preached by the apostles, first to the Jew and then to the Gentile. This is where discussion of the Seven Mountains becomes essential. Like the early disciples, we have been entrusted with this same commission. Matthew 28:18-20 calls us to disciple the nations while Mark 16:15-18 reminds us that the gospel of the Kingdom is for all creation, accompanied by God's power at work through His people. Together, these passages remind us of our great responsibility: to bring God's Kingdom to earth and to restore His family to Him.

This is why I so deeply appreciate the way Laurie Skipper lays out the Seven Mountain strategy in this book. I have heard it said that the Seven Mountain message is really about a plan for reforming cities and regions as part of the Great Commission. Laurie takes that big picture and makes it both practical and accessible. She does not overcomplicate the message. Instead, she gives us a clear, no-nonsense path to understand not only the "why" but also the "how" of engaging culture wherever God has placed us.

What stood out to me is how she focuses on transformation from a Kingdom perspective. It is not about retreating into safe spaces but stepping out as God's sons and daughters into business, education, government, media, the arts, family, and religion – wherever He has called us – to carry His presence and bring His influence. That is how the Kingdom advances.

I found myself encouraged, challenged, and equipped as I read. Laurie's step-by-step action plan helped me imagine what this can look like in everyday life, not just in theory. It gave me hope that transformation is not just possible, it is already in motion when we say yes to partnering with God in our places of assignment.

I wholeheartedly commend this book. It carries the heart of the Kingdom, the weight of Scripture, and the practicality we need to live it out. Thank you, Laurie, for giving us such a timely resource – and for reminding us that the Kingdom truly is at hand, ready to be lived and shared. I cannot wait to see this used as a reference at Kingdom University.

Dr. Howard K. Long
Dean, College of Kingdom Studies, Kingdom University

******

We agree that the restoration of all things comes from the Body of Christ retaking The Seven Mountains. It is in these high places that Christ gave us this authority. If we can understand who God created us to be, we will influence and advance the Kingdom of God. This is a must-read for this generation and the generations to come!

Apostle Matthew & Pastor Dena Hudson
Living Word Outreach, Wichita, KS

******

The Seven Mountain Mandate: Taking Your Place of Influence by Laurie Skipper presents a critical mandate to the body of Christ. Laurie has taken several Christian thinkers, authors, and reformers' revelations about this subject and, through her in-depth study, has brought them together collectively in a new light and a challenging framework for the body of Christ.

In this book, she mentions the early works of William Wilberforce (a British politician and philanthropist) and Abraham Kuyper (a Neo-Calvinist pastor who also served as prime minister of the Netherlands) within the seven spheres of culture. Next, she provides the collective revelation and thoughts of Loren Cunningham, Bill

Bright, and Francis Schaeffer on the subject. She then extensively discusses the work of present-day reformers Lance Wallnau and Johnny Enlow. The conclusion of these reformers' collective revelation is that cultural transformation in the Seven Spheres (Seven Mountains) occurs when righteousness and justice become the guiding principles, from a Biblical, Kingdom of God perspective. She mentions Wallnau's and Enlow's consistent emphasis on the transformation of culture, society, cities, and nations.

Along with the revelation of these reformers, she adds that as the church is being "re-formed" and we come out of our incorrect doctrines and mindsets, then change can bring us into proper alignment with God's plan and His Word. Finally, she puts the high challenge before the present-day body of Christ: "Where am I and where am I going?"

This is a must-read book for those who are consumed with God's agenda and purpose to bring about a drastic change beyond the four walls of our congregational gatherings.

Gautam Silal
President, Asian Mission Outreach, India

******

I thank God for enabling Laurie Skipper to author *The Seven Mountain Mandate: Taking Your Place of Influence*. This book will help believers understand how they can use their gifts to fulfill the Seven Mountain Mandate. Laurie's heart to teach the body of Christ on how to apply their gifts in their area of influence will be a blessing to many. I recommend that everyone read this book!

Prathyash Thomas
Hope to Nations International Ministry

******

The words within these pages bring a confluence of historical and prophetic insight into the plan of God. It provides a roadmap pointing the way of the Lord and a tool to equip an arising generation to be Kingdom Builders by taking their place of influence within the mountain(s) to which they are called.

David & Teresa Jones
Pastors, Banner Church, Tallahassee , FL

******

I am excited to share that this book delves into the fascinating dynamics of the Seven Mountains that influence our culture! Since 2007, I have had the privilege of hearing Lance Wallnau speak many times, and I will never forget discovering the inspiring mission Yahweh entrusted to him – to transform the Seven Mountains through the powerful influence of the Kingdom of God. Join me on this enlightening journey!

In 2004, the Holy Spirit, through a dream given to my wife, Cheryl, called us to begin influencing the Government Mountain. Many people, both within and outside the body of Christ, tried to discourage us, suggesting that I should not get involved in politics. Others pointed to the idea of separation of church and state. My response to anyone who says that is, "God established government; He wants to be involved in it through His people."

From 2010 through 2014, I was fortunate to labor alongside a friend who was both a representative in the Florida legislature and a Baptist pastor. We collaborated closely, and he attended many of the twelve-hour Solemn Assemblies that I hosted. During these gatherings, we prayed for the Government Mountain, and he was committed to praying, fasting, and seeking our Lord for Florida's government. I have also spent many hours in our state capitol, praying and lobbying whenever possible to be a positive influence on Florida's government. I have witnessed firsthand that the more we involve our Lord in the government affairs of our society the more we see the transformation of that government.

We are currently witnessing how Yahweh is challenging each mountain through His people with the good news of the gospel of the kingdom. Will you take your position? For too long, we have remained in the comfort of our churches and homes, prioritizing peace over action. Now is your time to arise and, like Josiah, make a change in history.

I recommend Laurie's book, *The Seven Mountain Mandate: Taking Your Place of Influence*, and encourage you to get involved.

Ken Malone, Forerunner Ministries, Satellite Beach, FL

The Seven Mountain Mandate

Taking Your Place of Influence

Laurie E. Skipper

Copyright

The Seven Mountain Mandate

by Laurie E. Skipper

Copyright © 2026 by Ekklesia Publishing

All rights reserved. This book is protected by the copyright laws of the United States of America. This book may not be copied or reprinted for commercial gain or profit. The use of short quotations or occasional page copying for personal or group study is encouraged. Permission will be granted upon request from Ekklesia Publishing.

All Scripture quotations, unless otherwise indicated, are taken from the New King James Version, © 1982 by Thomas Nelson, Inc.

Scripture quotations marked TPT are taken from The Passion Translation, © 2022 BroadStreet® Publishing Group, LLC. All Rights Reserved.

Scripture quotations marked NIV are taken from the New International Version, © 1973, 1978, 1984, 2011 by Biblica, Inc.

Scripture quotations marked AMP are taken from the Amplified Bible, © 1954, 1958, 1962, 1964, 1965, 1987 by The Lockman Foundation.

Scripture quotations marked NLT are taken from the New Living Translation, © 1996 by Tyndale House Publishers, Inc.

ISBN: 978-1-968924-00-3

Edit/Layout by Jim Bryson (JamesLBryson@gmail.com)

Graphics by David Munoz (davidmunoznvtn@gmail.com)

Table of Contents

Acknowledgements

I would first like to thank Drs. Greg and Joan Hood for following God's direction to found Kingdom University (KU). God directed me to KU to fulfill a life-long dream of completing a doctorate. Little did I realize that His plan all along was for me to do this work around my passion, the Kingdom of God. It is because of KU's doctoral requirement of developing and submitting a publishable manuscript that I am publishing my first book. That is something I have known for a long time that I would eventually do; publishing this fulfills yet another dream and portion of my destiny.

Next, I would like to thank the two men from whom I have learned so much about the Seven Mountain message. In the order in which I encountered their ministry, they are Dr. Lance Wallnau and Johnny Enlow. I do not know either personally. Yet, without the understanding they each brought and their deposits into my spirit, writing on this topic would not have been possible.

Finally, I would like to thank my friend, Jerry Wickline. While I had already known for years that I would eventually write and publish books, Jerry prophesied it to me back in the early 2000s. After that word, I would rarely see him that he did not ask, "When are you publishing that book?" Since Jerry has graduated to the great cloud of witnesses, I would like to extend my thanks to his beloved wife, Dr. Ruthie Wickline, as well as to Jerry's memory. While our paths only intersected for a few years, I will always value their friendship and appreciate their work for the Kingdom.

Foreword

In the same way, let your light shine before others, that they may see your good deeds and glorify your Father in heaven. (Matthew 5:16, NIV)

In a world marked by rapid change and noticeable unrest, the call for revival resonates louder than ever. It is a call not just for a deepened understanding of faith, but for a profound and transformative awakening that permeates the very fabric of our cultures. Laurie Skipper's new book, *The Seven Mountain Mandate: Taking Your Place of Influence*, is a clarion call to the Ekklesia – a challenge and an invitation to step into its God-given influence that should be shaping our society.

As we stand at the threshold of profound transformation, this new work invites you to engage with the pivotal question: What does it mean for America and our world to be truly saved? The Seven Mountains concept – encompassing religion, family, education, government, media, arts and entertainment, and business – serves as a framework for understanding the Ekklesia's role and responsibilities in everyday society. It reminds us that our mission extends beyond the walls of our buildings, reaching into every arena of life where culture is shaped and formed. Each mountain represents an area of influence where God's principles of righteousness and justice should reign; yet, too often, we see these spheres overtaken by secular ideologies and cultural chaos.

A rebellious nation is thrown into chaos, but leaders anointed with wisdom will restore law and order. (Proverbs 28:2, TPT)

As evidenced by the stirring movements on college campuses across the nation, we are witnessing a generation awakening to the profound truths of the Gospel of the Kingdom. The reports of thousands of young people seeking God and experiencing transformation are both encouraging and stirring. Yet the critical concern remains: How can we ensure these revivals lead to lasting change? History teaches us that the sustainability of a spiritual awakening always hinges on our commitment to engaging with the culture around us.

The revitalization of the Ekklesia is a critical first step, but it must be connected with a calculated strategy to influence the cultural mountains. In her book, Laurie Skipper unpacks the Seven Mountain Mandate with clarity and insight, offering both theological grounding and practical steps for believers. Each chapter unfolds a revelation that invites thought and action, inviting you, the reader, to evaluate your own area of influence within these key areas of life. It is a challenging journey – one that calls for a re-evaluation of how we engage with the world around us. The invitation to impact is not merely for the few who have specific titles or platforms; it is for every born-again, born-from-above believer who desires to see God's kingdom come on earth as it is in heaven.

Throughout the chapters, Laurie highlights the necessity of the five-fold equipping gifts (Ephesians 4:11) operating within these mountains. This vital perspective defines how the Ekklesia can more effectively mobilize itself to address society's various needs. Each mountain has its own unique challenges, yet the common thread remains: the need for Spirit-filled believers who mirror Christ's character and embody His mission. When the five-fold gifts flow into each sphere, believers are empowered to bring hope, truth, and transformation, rejuvenating the social, political, and cultural landscapes.

Furthermore, our understanding of revival must evolve. For the Ekklesia to say "America shall be saved" is not just a prophetic declaration; it is a commitment to seeing God's principles legislated in every sector of society. Laurie's breakdown of the disconnect between self-identified Christians and the moral decay around us challenges us to evaluate how we wield influence. We must advance from mere numbers to a movement marked by deep commitment, transformative action, and genuine engagement. The potential impact of embracing the Seven Mountain Mandate cannot be overstated. When the body of Christ corporately recognizes and acts upon its calling to influence, we will see cities, regions, and nations transformed.

Those of us who lean into this mandate can become conduits of God's love, truth, and justice – transforming the culture around us into one that mirrors the heart of our Father and King. So, as you delve into this book, I encourage you to open your heart and mind to the possibilities that await. Every chapter is infused with insights that can shift your mindset and awaken a sense of urgency. This book is not a passive reading experience; it is an opportunity to engage with the convictions that God has placed within you. How can you contribute to the mission of redeeming the various mountains and restoring society to its rightful alignment with God's kingdom? This book is not just a call to individual believers, but a call to the entire Ekklesia. We must come together to rise and reclaim our rightful places of influence.

> *This is what the Lord says: "I will restore the fortunes of Jacob's tents and have compassion on his dwellings; the city will be rebuilt on her ruins, and the palace will stand in its proper place. From them will come songs of thanksgiving and the sound of rejoicing. I will add to their numbers, and they will not be decreased; I will bring them honor, and they will not be disdained." (Jeremiah 30:18-19, NIV)*

For too long, we have allowed the narrative of culture to be written by those who do not defend or adhere to God's truths. The time has come for God's people to infuse every system with His will, confront injustices head-on, and usher in a new era of hope and transformation. *The Seven Mountain Mandate: Taking Your Place of Influence* is a manual for those who dare to dream of a world renewed under God's rulership. It serves as a compass for the Ekklesia not only to respond to revival but also to lead reformation and transformation across all facets of society. I invite you to journey through these pages, engage with the profound concepts introduced, and allow Holy Spirit to stir your heart with a fresh vision for your life and your community. May you be inspired to step into your place of influence and embrace the calling that God has on your life, recognizing that the future of our nation – and indeed the world – can change as we actively participate in His redemptive work. Let us rise to the occasion, armed with the knowledge that we indeed serve a God who desires to restore, redeem, and revolutionize every sphere of our existence. Together, we can shape our world into a reflection of his kingdom – where love, truth, justice, and mercy reign supreme.

> *Righteousness and justice are the foundation of your throne; love and faithfulness go before you. (Psalms 89:14, NIV)*

As you undertake this journey through *The Seven Mountain Mandate: Taking Your Place of Influence*, remember that you are not just reading a book; you are stepping into a movement that can and will change the landscape of our culture. May God empower you and guide you as you influence the mountains before you.

> *Then Jesus came close to them and said, "All authority of the universe has been given to me. Now wherever you go, make disciples of all nations, baptizing them in the name of the Father, the Son, and the Holy Spirit. And teach them to follow all that I have commanded you faithfully. And never forget that I am with you every day, even to the completion of this age." (Matthew 28:18-20, TPT)*

Greg Hood, Ph.D., Th.D.

President of Kingdom University
Apostolic Leader at Kingdom Life Network and Kingdom Life Ekklesia, Franklin, Tennessee
Author of: *The Gospel of the Kingdom*, *Seed Wars*, *Ancient Evil: Present-Day Manifestations Vol. 1 - The Rise of the Ekklesia*, and other books
www.GregHood.org

Preface

The initial intent for authoring this book was to fulfill requirements for completion of my doctorate at Kingdom University (KU). The school's preference was that research be combined with revelation to produce a book that could be used as part of the study curriculum at Kingdom University. In my four years of coursework at KU, the concept of the "Seven Mountains" or "seven spheres of cultural influence" was often mentioned, yet there was no course that addressed exactly what was meant nor why it is important. Having studied this area from a personal perspective, I selected it as my topic. My goal was to do a deep dive into its history and clearly explain its concepts and terminology while also providing fresh revelation regarding the message.

I was introduced to this teaching in the early 2000s and have followed its development and evolution for more than two decades. With that background, I felt I could produce a work that would bring historical understanding to this concept as well as add value by addressing a dimension that I had not seen addressed. Specifically, I introduce the function of the five-fold ministry gifts and how they each relate to the Seven Mountains. In addition, I provide definitions for each of the Seven Mountains, provide a step-by-step action plan for the Seven Mountain strategy, highlight the core Biblical principles that must be maintained, and provide a self-assessment guide.

Because of my intent for the book, the first section addresses five things, and the second section focuses on two. In Section 1, I tell the history of how this concept was brought back to the forefront. I then discuss the two primary ambassadors of the message. This brings understanding of the message and the terms used, including a discussion about each Mountain. I also synergize the differences in how the message developed and is presented by those two ambassadors. Finally, I outline the action steps needed to retake a territory, including providing the related, overarching Kingdom principles.

In Section 2, I first explain the role of the five-fold ministry gifts identified in Ephesians 4:11 and how they interact with each of the seven spheres of society. Then I issue a challenge to get engaged. To assist in doing that, I provide questions to ask oneself to get started or assess where you are.

In addition to providing the history of the message, this book will bring further clarification and new illumination by:

- providing a clear synopsis of each sphere or Mountain.
- providing a synergy of the differences between the way the messages developed and are presented by the two primary ambassadors of the message.
- providing an action list with overarching Kingdom principles for taking a sphere of influence.
- bringing understanding of the role of the five-fold ministry gifts within this message.
- providing a checklist for getting started or assessing where you are in your sphere of influence.

The reader will gain a deeper understanding of this message and then be challenged to incorporate it into their lifestyle to further advance the Kingdom of God.

Introduction

Today we are hearing a lot of talk about revival. There are those who say it is coming, while others believe it has already started, especially on college campuses and among young adults. That it has begun is evidenced by not only what happened at Asbury University in February 2023, but with what is continuing to happen on other college campuses, including state universities. Speaking from the University of Arkansas in September 2024, a CBN report stated:

> As CBN News has reported, this UniteUS event was one of a series bringing the Gospel message to college campuses across the country.
>
> Tonya Prewitt, founder of UniteUS, explained, "We started at Auburn University. We had 5,000 students show up, and over 200 got baptized. We next went to FSU – Florida State, the second biggest party school in the nation. We had 4,500 students come, and I believe about 350 students got baptized at that event."
>
> The movement then swept through the universities of Alabama, Georgia, Tennessee, and South Carolina, with numbers growing along the way. Tonya calls the mission a simple one: Bring hope to a generation.[1]

In a larger article about the event at the University of Arkansas, they also talked about what had happened at the University of South Carolina, Texas A&M University, and Ohio State University.[2] And it is continuing. A CBN headline from 2025 reported, "'They Want God': 8,000 Students Seek Jesus in Huge Kentucky Revival, 2,000 Give Lives to Christ."[3] Another one reported, "5,000 Students Seek

Jesus at WVU, Nearly 1,000 Respond to Altar Call: 'Life-Changing Salvation.'"[4]

After a UniteUS event at the University of Central Florida in February 2026, Crosswalk reported, "The movement of God on college campuses that began in fall 2023 and continued through 2024 and 2025 showed no signs of slowing down Tuesday night."[5] Their article said over 5,000 students attended, with 1,600 making decisions for Christ and hundreds being baptized. They noted that since the first UniteUS rally in September 2023, "more than 140,000 students have taken part in similar gatherings nationwide, from Florida to Ohio to Arizona."

A CBN article in April 2026 reported, "Another powerful move of the Holy Spirit erupted this week at Florida State University in Tallahassee as the spiritual awakening on America's college campuses isn't showing signs of slowing down."[6] They quoted UniteUS' Instagram post saying, "Students who gave their lives to Jesus in 2024 stepped up to lead at Unite FSU 2026! God continues to move at FSU!" (@unite_us, April 1, 2026). God is on the move among Generation Z. May it spread to all generations!

However, there is a strong warning that if revival does not lead to awakening and awakening to reformation, it will be short-lived. One does not have to be prophetic to see that; one must only study history. Revival, in and of itself, does not bring transformation to a city or nation. It did not in Lakeland, Brownsville, or Toronto. Nor did the Jesus People Movement of the late 1960s and 1970s, which spread across the nation, bring transformation to the United States, not even to Southern California, where it started and remained centered. Were people born again and their lives transformed? Yes. Did it transform their culture? No. They filled local churches, many of which grew tremendously; new churches were birthed; and both the genre of Contemporary Christian Music and a new era of worship music were born. That had a significant effect on the Church realm, but it had no effect on the rest of society. How do we ensure that this revival does not go the same path of saving people but not saving our nation?

What do we even mean when we say, "*America shall be saved*"? That phrase has become a mantra to many in the Pentecostal and charismatic realms (especially within the apostolic-prophetic realm) of the Church in America, many of whom have heard it from Dutch Sheets, though it did not originate with him. What does it mean? What are we saying?

It does not simply mean, "a lot of people in the United States will be saved." According to a recent report by the Pew Research Center, "62% of U.S. adults describe themselves as Christians,"[7] with this number leveling off since 2019 after decades of decline. (Pew reports that it was around 90 percent in 1990.[8]) If we have over half the population saying they are Christian and the country could be saved by having enough Christians, why is it in the current state? Why have we seen such a tremendous moral and ethical decline? How have Socialist and Marxist ideologies infiltrated our culture, if we win by simply having the majority?

Those changes have not been brought by *having the most people* but rather by *having people with the most influence*. It is influence we must regain. The question becomes, "How do we regain the influence?" That is where the Seven Mountain message brings revelation needed for reformation. First, as the body of Christ, we must reform by changing what we believe (to align with the revelation). Then we must take action based on those beliefs to reform and bring transformation to our cities and nations. To answer the initial question:

America shall be saved when …

- she has been influenced by the sons and daughters of God …
    - who are operating out of the Kingdom principles Jesus taught …

- resulting in a cultural transformation in all seven spheres …
  - in which the guiding principles become righteousness and justice from a Biblical, Kingdom of God perspective.

That will mean that laws are changed to align with that perspective and true justice (laced with mercy) is meted out. To accomplish that, *every* segment of society must be discipled with Kingdom principles and transformed.

The Seven Mountain message has come to the forefront from two perspectives. One was seeking *how to disciple nations*. The other was seeking *how to see the transformation of cities and nations*. It turns out, the solution to both is found in this same message. **The goal of the Seven Mountain message is to see nations transformed by teaching the principles Jesus taught.**

Why? Because Jesus was promised nations for His inheritance. (See Psalm 2:8.) After His resurrection and just before He ascended, Jesus gave the clear instruction that we were to disciple nations, teaching them to observe all that He had commanded us. (See Matthew 28:19-20.) According to Matthew 25:31-46, when Jesus returns, one of the first things He will do is separate the nations, sheep versus goat, and send each to their reward.

> [31] *"When the Son of Man comes in His glory, and all the holy angels with Him, then He will sit on the throne of His glory.* [32] *All the nations will be gathered before Him, and He will separate them one from another, as a shepherd divides his sheep from the goats.* [33] *And He will set the sheep on His right hand, but the goats on the left.* [34] *Then the King will say to those on His right hand, 'Come, you blessed of My Father, inherit the kingdom prepared for you from the foundation of the world: …'* [41] *Then He will also say to those on the left hand, 'Depart from Me, you cursed, into the everlasting fire prepared for the*

> *devil and his angels. ...'* [46] *And these will go away into everlasting punishment, but the righteous into eternal life." (Matthew 25:31-34, 41, 46)*

Most of us have only thought of *individuals* being "saved" or "lost" and entering eternal reward or punishment, not *nations*. Yet, Jesus clearly said *nations*. (This, of course, does not replace the role of personal salvation and judgment.) Our responsibility to disciple nations affects how large His inheritance will be. If the Church does her job well, there will be far more sheep nations than goat nations. Our actions help determine which nations will inherit His Kingdom with Him and gain eternal life, versus which nations will be condemned to everlasting torment intended only for the devil and his angels.

The reason that we must disciple nations is that 1) Jesus told us to in Matthew 28:19 (which is enough) and 2) His inheritance (and, per Romans 8:17, ours) depends on it. We will see that it is in their discipling that they are transformed. It is in understanding and executing this message of bringing the *influence* of the Kingdom of God into the different spheres of society that brings *transformation*. Now that we understand where we are going, let us explore how to get there.

This book is structured to first bring understanding to a concept that is referred to by different terms. It has been called the "seven spheres of influence in society" and the "seven spheres of cultural influence." The term I prefer is "seven mountains." The common thread is that all of these refer to the same seven *things*.

To highlight the term, I have chosen hereafter to capitalize "Seven Mountains" and the names of each of the individual Mountains (e.g., Media, Family) wherever they appear. Likewise, I capitalize the term "Mountain" itself when used to refer to one of the Seven Mountains. The exception to this will be in a direct quote, where capitalization will remain as it is in the source. I have also chosen to capitalize the word "Church" when it refers to the global body of Christ and "Kingdom" when it is referring to the Kingdom of God.

When speaking of the generic roles, such as the five-fold ministry gifts of apostle, prophet, evangelist, pastor, and teacher, or any other generic role, I will refer to the person filling that role as simply "he" rather than using "(s)he" or "he/she" each time. Of course, women fill these roles as well. Since men are part of the "Bride of Christ" and ladies are counted among both the "Sons of God" and the "brethren," I trust you will allow this latitude.

Section 1 identifies and defines those seven *things* to bring understanding to the concept. This section presents the history of the message. It discusses those to whom it was revealed and how the revelation came, as well as some who implemented it without ever formalizing the concept. It introduces those who became the primary ambassadors of the message through teaching as well as practicing its principles. It looks at each mountain, describing and defining each one. The last chapter in this section is a recap of the journey of the two primary ambassadors of the message, synergizing the key differences in how each of their messages evolved and was presented. It provides a summarized action list for regaining these spheres with the overarching Kingdom principles that must be followed in doing so.

Section 2 addresses how the five-fold ministry gifts identified in Ephesians 4:11 relate to each of the Mountains. It then urges the reader to determine the place he or she was created to fill and begin to work purposefully toward fulfilling that portion of their personal destiny. A checklist is provided to aid in getting started. It is my belief that as we each fulfill what we were created to do, the sum of the whole will bring great advancement to the Kingdom of God on earth and, eventually, "The kingdoms of this world [will] become the kingdoms of our Lord and of His Christ" as stated in Revelation 11:15.

If you are not familiar with the concept of the Seven Mountains, I believe you will find the first section highly informative. If you are already familiar with the concept, I urge you not to skip it. In doing so, you might miss some nuggets of truth or a deeper understanding of the message. Either way, my hope is that the last section does two things.

First, I hope it brings encouragement to those who have already identified their role and are working to secure their highest level of calling. Second, I hope it challenges anyone who has not yet whole-heartedly embraced this mandate from God.

The challenge is to find our place and begin to advance the Kingdom of God with new boldness within our sphere of influence. It is a call to join – or to continue in – the battle for the reformation.

It is an exciting time to be alive. Reformation, both in the Church and in society, has begun, though most do not yet realize it. The forerunners and early adopters of this message have been those who have been used to kindle the fire that is starting this reformation. I hope to convince you to join their ranks if you have not yet done so. We must continue the push to see everything "re-formed" and "re-aligned" to God's initial design and intent.

Section 1

The Message and the Messengers

Chapter 1
The Seven Mountain Mandate

The Mountains

Before we begin to delve into a bit of history of how this concept began to be understood and taught, we need to first understand what we mean by the term. As discussed in the Introduction, some call these the "seven spheres of influence in society." Others call them the "seven spheres of cultural influence." Loren Cunningham of Youth With A Mission called them the "mind-molders." Bill Bright of Campus Crusade for Christ called them "world systems." Even the secular world has picked up the concept. Charlie Kirk, founder of Turning Point USA, called them the "seven verticals" or "seven pillars." (Think: the pillars on which society rests.) The term I prefer is "Seven Mountains," though I will interchangeably refer to them as "spheres." My preference is driven in part because the pictorial reference of the mountains helps visualize, and visualization aids understanding and retention of the concept. The mountain concept comes from Isaiah 2:2:

Now it shall come to pass in the latter days
That the mountain of the Lord's house
Shall be established on the top of the mountains,
And shall be exalted above the hills;
And all nations shall flow to it.

Here we see that the Lord's house is built on a mountain which is located "on the top of" other mountains. I believe the mountain which is "on the top of" the other mountains is the "great and high mountain" referenced in Revelation 21:10.

Different people who have grasped and taught this same basic concept have used different terminology and have at times identified the items in the list of seven slightly differently. Some of those differences will be addressed in the following chapter. As the teaching has matured over time, the following list of the seven areas of influence has emerged consistently with two minor variations. They are:

- Media
- Family
- Arts & Entertainment or Celebration
- Economy or Business
- Religion
- Education
- Government

The order of the list varies, and some prefer the term "Business" rather than "Economy" and "Celebration" rather than "Arts & Entertainment." In looking deeper at how these are used, we find that it is mostly an issue of preference in the choice of a term for the category.

The critical issue is not what they are called. The issue is understanding each sphere and how to influence it for the sake of the Kingdom of God. There are at least a couple of people of late wanting to make a category for "Science & Technology." I disagree with that for two reasons. First, the list was created by revelation from God to at least four different people. That is reason enough for me. Additionally, having worked in the Technology arena for nearly forty years, I very much agree with including it in the Business sphere as has been done. Business cannot exist without it.

The Mandate & The Problem with Terminology

The mandate is that we, the followers of Christ, disciple nations. We will learn that to do that, we must go into each of these areas within our society and permeate it with the influence of the Kingdom of God. Within the Church, we often talk in terms of warfare and conquering, drawing analogies to the children of Israel conquering their Promised Land and all the subsequent battles to continue to occupy it. However, that rhetoric is often used against us by those who do not understand our underlying beliefs. They like to make it seem that we are calling for violence or a violent overthrow. We understand that we are not; that is not the way we advance the Kingdom of God.

> *The mandate is that we, the followers of Christ, disciple nations.*

We know, "The weapons we fight with are not the weapons of the world. On the contrary, they have divine power to demolish strongholds," (2 Corinthians 10:4, NIV). The New Living Translation (NLT) puts it this way: "We use God's mighty weapons, not worldly weapons, to knock down the strongholds of human reasoning and to destroy false arguments." It is "God's mighty weapons" that will "knock down the strongholds of human reasoning," even those that have seemed impenetrable. That will allow each area to begin to operate under the influence of King Jesus and His principles. His way is the only way to experience true freedom, peace, and prosperity.

We understand our battles are done in prayer and the only way we take over is through developing influence that supersedes the influence of others. To get to that level of influence, we must first get into the game by entering these spheres. Only then will we be able to effectively use "God's mighty weapons" in prayer and develop the level of influence necessary to shift the culture and see "[His] kingdom come, [His] will be done on earth as it is in heaven," (Matthew 6:10).

This takeover is never by force; it is always by influence.

Likewise, there is often talk of "taking the tops of the Mountains." Again, this terminology can be very misunderstood. We know it is about taking them by *influence*, not by force. Yet, we very much need to take them – meaning to become key influencers at the tops of each of the Mountains.

Johnny Enlow started the closing chapter in *The Seven Mountain Prophecy,* quoting Deuteronomy 28:13: "And the Lord will make you the head and not the tail; you shall be above only, and not be beneath, if you heed the commandments of the Lord your God, which I command you today, and are careful to observe them." He then stated:

> It is important that we, God's blood-bought people, realize that it has always been His will for us to be at the top of the mountains in a place of preeminence and blessing. He is not a sadistic God who loves seeing His people struggle and barely survive. Nothing could be further from the truth. He has always sought to motivate us with a promised land of unlimited abundance – body, soul, and spirit.[9]

For true Kingdom-minded people, this takeover is *never by force*; it is *always by influence*. Further, for the true disciple of Christ, being at the top does not mean *ruling over* people; rather, it means *being a servant of* the people. (See Mark 9:34-35.) It is about demonstrating righteousness and shedding the light of God. Light will always dispel darkness, but it takes more than a single candle at the top to take the Mountain. We need lights of righteousness shining all up and down the mountain. We will not begin to reform our nation (or any nation) until we understand that and begin to act upon it.

Most definitions you will find in a web search for "Seven Mountain Mandate" are written by individuals with limited first-hand knowledge, incorrect assumptions, and quotes taken out of context. Realize that if you accept the Seven Mountain Mandate and begin living it, you will be accused of believing things that you do not believe and assigned motives that you never even considered. *If you are going to be a reformer, get used to it!*

Reformation always has strong opposition and not just from unbelievers. The most painful attacks will come from your brothers and sisters in Christ who do not wish to move into the "new thing" that God is doing. Check Church history. *Reformers always pay a price.* Count the cost before you sign up. Then, remember, "We use God's mighty weapons, not worldly weapons, to knock down the strongholds of human reasoning and to destroy false arguments."

It is our job to disciple nations by teaching them His ways

Do We Have a Mandate?

Do we have a mandate to spread the influence of the Kingdom of God throughout every area of our culture? Are we all called to do this? Yes. It came directly from Jesus, just before His ascension. In Matthew 28:19-20, He said:

> *19 "Go therefore and make disciples of all the nations, baptizing them in the name of the Father and of the Son and of the Holy Spirit, 20 teaching them to observe all things that I have commanded you; and lo, I am with you always, even to the end of the age."*

Jesus instructed them – and us – to "make *disciples* of all *nations … teaching them to observe all things* that I have commanded you." Put simply, *it is our job to disciple nations by teaching them His ways*, which means bringing His culture into every area of society.

It is obvious that, even with a majority saying they are Christians, our nation is not observing the teachings of Christ in any of these areas (including a sizeable portion of the Church). Let us move now into how this mandate was re-introduced to the body of Christ fifty years ago and has been taught for the past twenty-five years. Yet, mainstream Christianity has still not accepted it. As reformers, it is our job to help make that so. This is a key component of the reformation of the Church. But first we must understand the Seven Mountain Mandate and become personally convinced of its truths and our responsibility to obey it.

Chapter 2

The Message Revealed

Three People, One Revelation

Most who are familiar with the Seven Mountain Mandate concept trace the modern-day roots of the message back to two gentlemen, each the head of a large evangelical organization. Holy Spirit revealed to each of them, almost simultaneously, a list of seven areas that must be impacted to fulfill the Great Commission in Matthew 28:18-20 to "make disciples of all the nations." Those men were Loren Cunningham, founder of Youth With A Mission (YWAM), and Bill Bright, founder of Campus Crusade for Christ. As the story has been told and retold, there are many variations of the meeting in which the two of them realized they had each received *the same revelation the day before their meeting*. What follows is a synopsis of an interview in which Loren Cunningham shared the story with Kelle Ortiz and Os Hillman in 2007.[10]

In August 1975, Cunningham and his family were vacationing in the mountains of Colorado. He had for some time been seeking the Lord about how to disciple nations. One day, while vacationing, the Lord gave him a list of seven things he had never considered and told him, "This is the way to reach America and nations for God."[11] Cunningham called them "mind-molders" or "spheres."

Later that day, a friend called to tell him that their mutual friends, Bill and Vonette Bright, were also visiting Colorado and would love to see the Cunninghams while they were there. The following day, Loren and Darlene Cunningham flew to visit the Brights. As they greeted each other, Cunningham reached for the paper on which he had written this list of "mind-molders." As he did, Bill Bright exclaimed, "Loren, I want to show you what God has shown me!"[12] According to Cunningham, "It was virtually the same list God had given me the day before."[13] Bright was calling them the "world systems."

In the interview, Cunningham identified the seven "mind-molders" as:

- Family
- Church or the people of God
- School or Education
- Media, Public Communication, in all forms, printed and electronic
- Celebration including the arts, entertainment, and sports
- Economy which starts with innovations in science and technology, productivity, sales, and service (which is often called Business)
- Government

He particularly emphasized the need to consider the Economy or Business realm, starting with innovations in science and technology. He viewed innovation as the key to generating wealth at any level and noted that we tend to leave out the scientific part, which raises the wealth of the world.

The story gets even better. Three weeks later, Cunningham's wife saw Dr. Francis Schaeffer on television talking about the same list! Learning that this well-known, evangelical theologian was teaching this same message, Cunningham realized this was not just a revelation for YWAM and Campus Crusade for Christ. Nor was it just for the youth or the "next generation" as he initially believed. He realized God was restoring a revelation to the Church of how to disciple nations.

No doubt Cunningham's views and teachings about these spheres had grown over the thirty-two years between the initial revelation and this interview. At YWAM, he had established the University of the Nations (UofN) with courses to train those going as missionaries, as he referred to them, into each of the seven spheres. He called those purposefully going into the secular spheres "missionaries," just like we do those sent to spread the gospel in a different nation. And well they should be. Both are called to their assignment, and both should be advancing the Kingdom of God within the sphere to which they are assigned.

The gospel of the Kingdom is much larger, much more encompassing, than the gospel of salvation. Yet it is the gospel of salvation that we have typically preached both at home (in our own nation) and abroad (as missionaries to other nations). When Jesus told his disciples in Mark 16:15 to "Go into all the world and preach the gospel to every creature," they knew the gospel to which He referred was the gospel of the Kingdom. That was the message Jesus had preached consistently from the very beginning of his public ministry. This is reaffirmed in Matthew 24:14, "And *this gospel of the kingdom will be preached in all the world as a witness to all the nations*, and then the end will come." (Emphasis added.) Notice that it is to be a witness "to *all nations*," not "to *some people in each nation*."

While Bill Bright undoubtedly incorporated this new revelation of the need to impact these "world systems" into the Campus Crusade for Christ training, there is no place to easily find his teaching on this subject. He is best remembered as the author of *The Four Spiritual Laws* gospel tract. We should not forget, however, his contribution to the advancement of the Kingdom of God as one who received this revelation and passed it on. For example, The Pinnacle Forum, an organization whose motto is "Transforming Leaders, Who Transform Culture," was inspired by Bill Bright's message. They transitioned their materials to using the Seven Mountain paradigm to train leaders to impact their cities.

Francis Schaeffer's role in bringing this new revelation forward is not as well known or documented. He is recognized as an evangelical theologian, philosopher, and apologist, as well as being a Presbyterian pastor. He and his wife, Edith Schaeffer, cofounded the L'Abri community in Switzerland, which initially provided a forum for philosophical and religious discussions. It grew into a study and training center. There are seven residential branches of L'Abri operating today, with the center in Switzerland as well as centers in the Netherlands, England, South Korea, Canada, and two in the United States.

It was in 1975 that Schaeffer began to discuss the concept that would come to be known as the Seven Mountain Mandate. It is unclear how or when he came to understand this message. As far as we know, he first began to speak about it the same year it was revealed to Bright and Cunningham. Of the twenty-two books Schaeffer wrote, none were focused on this topic. Like Bill Bright, it is not clear how much this revelation impacted any of his subsequent teaching. We can only assume that it did. What we do know is that Francis and Edith Schaeffer were both very multi-cultural and saw Christ as belonging in *every area* of our lives, much like Abraham Kuyper, who will be discussed shortly.

While Cunningham, Bright, and Schaeffer are usually given the credit as the ones who introduced what has come to be known as the Seven Mountain Mandate, they were not the first to receive this revelation. As is often the case, God has forerunners who begin to re-introduce a lost truth before the masses are ready to hear it. For the Seven Mountain Mandate, two such forerunners were William Wilberforce and Abraham Kuyper. There is no evidence that either Wilberforce or Kuyper ever articulated "the seven spheres of society" or taught the Seven Mountain Mandate as we know and teach it today. Rather, they demonstrated the effectiveness of its principles. Each impacted his nation by reaching into each of the seven spheres of influence. We will look at each of these men briefly to understand their impacts.

William Wilberforce

William Wilberforce (1759 – 1833) was a British politician, philanthropist, evangelical Christian, and dedicated social reformer. When Wilberforce underwent what he called his "Great Change" at the age of twenty-six, he had already been serving in parliament for five years. In now fully surrendering his life to God, he believed that he must pull away from the world and focus solely on spiritual matters. This almost caused Wilberforce to resign from parliament, which would have cost him fulfilling the assignment for which he had been created.

"Surely the principles as well as the practice of Christianity are simple and lead not to meditation only but to action."

Fortunately, the efforts of Prime Minister William Pitt, who was Wilberforce's dearest friend, combined with those of a friend from the days of his childhood, Pastor John Newton, convinced him otherwise. Pitt admonished him that, "Surely the principles as well as the practice of Christianity are simple and lead not to meditation only but to action."[14] Meeting with Wilberforce to discuss his Great Change, John Newton urged him to stay in parliament. Newton later wrote him saying, "It is hoped and believed that the Lord has raised you up for the good of His church and for the good of the nation."[15] And so, He had. Thankfully, God is still in the business of raising up individuals for both purposes, even if they are not the ones we expect. One of them might be you!

Not long after his conversion, Wilberforce journaled, "God almighty has set before me two great objects: the suppression of the Slave Trade and the reformation of manners."[16] These became his passions (some would say obsessions), and a reformer was born. He and the Clapham Sect, of which he was a key member, are credited with not just ending the slave trade but causing the full abolition of slavery itself in the entire British Empire. In addition, they are credited with social reforms in numerous other areas of society. These included such things as:

- ending public hangings of criminals, which were often followed by public dismemberment.
- improved working conditions and hours in the factories for both children and adults.
- establishment of "Sunday schools" that met on Sunday afternoons to teach the children too poor to afford education how to read using the scriptures (simultaneously teaching them about God).
- founding of the Society for the Prevention of Cruelty to Animals to stop the extreme abuse of animals, often done just for sport.

The Clapham Sect consisted of individuals from each of the Mountains. They spread their message through newspapers, magazines, and flyers. They published stories and poems about it and created theatrical productions. They improved the education system and passed laws. They got funding from the businessmen to finance their endeavors. Though there is no evidence that the Seven Mountain concept was in their thinking, it is obvious that Holy Spirit led them to use its principles to accomplish God's intended agenda. They did not send people into each of these Mountains; they found like-minded people who were already there and began to band together.

By working together, they shifted the British culture from one of almost total debauchery into the Victorian era. If it was possible then, it is possible now, both in the UK and the US.

Abraham Kuyper

Abraham Kuyper (1837-1920) of the Netherlands had diverse interests, abilities, and involvements and he allowed his Christianity to shape his views and opinions in all areas of life. He was the son of a minister and earned a doctorate in theology. He became a very influential neo-Calvinist pastor, establishing the Reformed Churches in the Netherlands in 1892. It became the second largest Protestant denomination in the country behind the Dutch Reformed Church.

> *"... there is not a square inch in the whole domain of our human existence over which Christ, who is Sovereign over all, does not cry: 'Mine!'"*

He was elected to parliament in 1874, where he was particularly interested in the equal financing of public and religious schools. Additionally, in 1876, he authored a paper that laid the foundation for what would become a new political party, the Anti-Revolutionary Party. It was the protestant conservative and Christian democratic political party. He was the party's chairman from 1879 until 1905, but was recognized as the leader of the party until his death in 1920. He also served as prime minister from 1901 until 1905.

If that was not enough, during that same time, he founded the Free University (Vrije Universiteit Amsterdam), one of two publicly funded research universities in Amsterdam. Interestingly, he was also a journalist and kept that job even while serving in parliament. He was even chair of the Dutch Circle of Journalists in 1898. He also lectured at Princeton Theological Seminary, the Presbyterian Seminary at Princeton University, here in the United States.

If we look at it in terms of Mountains, at various times Kuyper either worked or participated in leadership in the Mountains of Religion, Government, Business, Education, and Media. As a husband and father of eight children, he would seem to have been involved in the Family Mountain. The one area in which he does *not* appear to have been involved was the realm of Arts & Entertainment, other than bringing it into his lectures at Princeton. There, he discussed the relationship of Calvinism (his view of Christianity) with philosophy, religion, politics, science, art, and the future.

In contrast to Wilberforce and his associates, Kuyper not only operated out of an understanding of the need to impact each of these areas of society, he also articulated Christianity's relationship to them to others. One of his most famous quotes sums up his philosophy:

> Oh, no single piece of our mental world is to be hermetically sealed off from the rest, and there is not a square inch in the whole domain of our human existence over which Christ, who is Sovereign over all, does not cry: "Mine!"[17]

Did you catch that? *Back in the late 1800s,* Abraham Kuyper was saying that *Christ laid claim to every area, "the whole domain of our human existence," every sphere in which we endeavor.* It then took more than seventy-five years for this truth to begin to resurface within the Church. It would be yet another twenty-five years – a full century later – before voices rose up to begin to bring this teaching to the forefront.

In Need of a Messenger

As previously discussed, Loren Cunningham, Bill Bright, and Francis Schaeffer are usually given the primary credit for today's Seven Mountain Mandate revelation. But not only were they not the first to operate with this revelation, they were not the ones to begin to teach and evangelize the message to the larger body of Christ. We should not minimize their role. God chose them as the vessels through whom to re-introduce this truth. Both Cunningham and Bright, each of whom led a missions-focused organization, had been seeking Him as to how to disciple nations. (Perhaps Schaeffer was as well; we do not know.) God responded to their persistent question. However, none of them brought the teaching to the Church at large.

In the next chapter, we will look at the individual that God raised up as the pioneer to mature the message and teach the concept revealed to Cunningham, Bright, and Schaeffer. It was time for the message to be heralded to the body of Christ at large, and God had been preparing a voice through whom to speak.

Chapter 3

The Message Gets a Voice

> The first stage of any powerful idea begins with theorists who generate ideas, moves to researchers who revise and validate ideas, moves to the teachers who popularize ideas, and finally reaches practitioners who translate those ideas into tangible models. ~ *Lance Wallnau*[18]

The quote above is from the Foreword, written by Lance Wallnau, in Michael Maiden's book, *Turn the World Upside Down: Discipling the Nations with the Seven Mountain Strategy*. Wallnau is one of the primary *researchers* and *teachers* for this message and a *practitioner*. Today, he is one of the most widely recognized and sought after speakers on the topic of the Seven Mountains and cultural transformation. He has shared this message as well as provided business consulting related to it around the world. The bio on his website says:

> Lance is the innovator who introduced the "Seven Mountains of Culture" as a fresh template to explain how the church must engage culture at the turn of the century.
>
> Dr. Wallnau is a strategist, futurist and compelling communicator who has shared platforms with Ben Carson, Mike Pompeo, and best-selling authors Ken Blanchard and John Maxwell. He has conducted training for the United Nations and spoken at Harvard, the Chinese Academy of Social Sciences, and the London School of Theology. With a thirty-year background consulting business and non-profits,

> Lance's students represent a global tapestry spanning governments, CEOs, entertainers, and entrepreneurs.
>
> He currently directs the Lance Learning Group, a strategic teaching and consulting company based in Dallas, Texas.[19]

Let us back up and look at a bit of his journey to get where he is today, especially with respect to the Seven Mountain message.

Hearing the Message

In 2000, Lance Wallnau was speaking at a conference in Canada at which Loren Cunningham was also speaking. Cunningham told him the story of his meeting with Bill Bright in 1975, when they realized that God had given each of them the same seven spheres of influence that would need to be penetrated to reach nations. Even with hearing the message from Francis Schaeffer and realizing it was for the body of Christ at large, each seems to have remained focused on teaching it to the young adults with whom they worked. It answered the question each had been asking God, "How do we disciple nations?" While acknowledging it as truth, they used it simply as a key given to them for use within their own evangelistic ministries. As far as can be determined, neither sought to expand their teaching of this revelation beyond their own organization and its sphere of influence.

This concept was new to Lance Wallnau when Loren Cunningham shared it with him. He has expressed wondering how this (to him) "momentous event" of the dual revelation of this concept to the two of them virtually simultaneously could have happened in 1975 and he was *just* hearing about it in 2000. God has His timing. Hearing the answer God had given these men to their question of how to disciple nations refocused Wallnau's message and mission. His mission became sharing this message and seeing it implemented.

Little did Loren Cunningham realize that he had just been used by God to ignite a fire that would become Wallnau's passion. The message of the Seven Mountain Mandate was about to meet its *kairos* moment. As Wallnau studied the Word and allowed Holy Spirit to develop the concept and embed it deep in his spirit, he began to teach it. It was Wallnau who transitioned the terminology from "mind-molders," "world systems," or "spheres" to "mountains." He is the one who first introduced that pictorial reference. Those who have attended his meetings are familiar with his whiteboard drawings of seven mountains with one large mountain overshadowing them.

Preparing the Messenger

God had spent decades preparing Lance Wallnau to be the carrier of the message. He did not set out to go into "full-time ministry" as we so often call it (or "vocational ministry" as C. Peter Wagner called it). Wallnau's father was a lawyer and businessman. He was expected to follow in his father's footsteps. And so, he did. Lance Wallnau pursued a career in the business realm. He worked as a consultant and coach with Human Resources personnel and senior levels of management in large, Fortune 500 companies.

> *Many wondering about the seemingly haphazard, unplanned path of their lives are nearing convergence where it will all make sense.*

His career was going very well, and he was prospering financially. *Until* his deepening experiences with God caused him to fall into the same line of thinking that had almost sidetracked William Wilberforce – if one truly surrenders one's life to God, one must pull away from the world and focus solely on spiritual matters. At the time, Wallnau was living in Babylon – Babylon, New York, that is, on Long Island. It seemed clear to him that God was "calling him out of Babylon" as he often puts it. (Prophets love double meanings.) Out of Babylon he came, figuratively and literally.

He walked away from a very lucrative and promising secular career to "go into ministry."

Wallnau would go from his humble beginnings as a worship leader in a small church that met over an automobile service garage to eventually being the senior pastor of a large and successful church in Rhode Island. However, because of requests from fellow ministers who were aware of his background, he began providing consulting to church leaders from the skills he acquired and honed during his secular career. Little did he know that God was beginning to nudge him into a new direction where he would find his life's call or, to use his term, his point of convergence. His definition and explanation of that term are included below because there are many for whom this may bring clarity to all you have been – or are still going – through. You are being prepared for convergence. Wallnau states that, statistically, convergence usually happens sometime after age 50. That means for some it may happen sooner and for others later. (For some of us, much later!) So do not give up hope if you have not yet reached yours.

> [Convergence is] when you are walking in fulfillment of what God has been preparing you for your whole life. … It's when you're walking in the prophetic script God wrote for you before you were born. The Convergence Zone is actually a place where your gifts and talents and acquired skills, over a lifetime, come together with your mistakes and your learning to create a kind of unique composition – to prepare you for a role that you step into that maximizes 100 percent of your latent potential. Meaning, you're now doing the thing you were created to do.[20]

Wallnau's training and experience in his secular career included being comfortable consulting and working with top-level leaders and people of influence. That, combined with what he gained while working in vocational ministry, including through his theological studies, gave him the knowledge and experience he needed. All of that blended with the natural talents and spiritual gifts that had been placed within him. Add the relational connections he had made along the way, and he was finally equipped to step into the purpose for which he had been created. He had reached convergence.

Many who have wondered about the seemingly haphazard, unplanned path their lives have taken are nearing their point of convergence where it will all come together and make sense. Do not grow weary and pull back now. Your point of convergence is coming. Hold on to the promise in Habakkuk 2:3:

For the vision is yet for an appointed time;
But at the end it will speak, and it will not lie.
Though it tarries, wait for it;
Because it will surely come,
It will not tarry.

Spreading the Message

God connected Wallnau with some of the major leaders and voices of the day within the apostolic-prophetic realm of the Church within America. Many of them provided an audience for the Seven Mountain message that would quickly grasp its significance and open doors for him to further spread the message. In the early 2000s, he did that mostly through conferences and seminars and the CDs and DVDs produced at them. It would be a decade before he committed the concept to paper for formal publication.

Wallnau's Seven Mountain Mandate message had gained the attention of leaders who saw the need for incorporating it as a portion of a larger message. It was Ché Ahn who succeeded in getting Wallnau to finally put pen to paper to explain the message. (Ché Ahn and his wife, Sue Ahn, are the founding pastors and apostolic leaders of Harvest Rock Church in Pasadena, California.) "The Seven

Mountain Mandate" was one of ten topics that Ahn wanted included in a book about reformation that he was developing as a compiling editor. Each topic was given its own chapter and written by the person Ahn perceived as anointed for that message. He reached out to his friend, Lance Wallnau, for this topic. The core of "The Seven Mountain Mandate" message as Wallnau had been teaching it was finally published in *The Reformer's Pledge*[21] in 2010. That chapter was republished in 2013 as a chapter of another book, *Invading Babylon: The 7 Mountain Mandate.*[22] That book was, likewise, a compilation of writings by different authors. I highly recommend both books.

How is it that Christianity has power to transform an individual's life yet we, as a people group, are impotent to influence our own nations?

Yet, after teaching this new truth for a decade and even finally committing it to print, in a post on his website some years later Wallnau confesses his frustration. He says he feels like Neo in *The Matrix* with questions that were like "a splinter in my brain."[23] Below are some of the questions that were plaguing him:

- How is it that Christianity has power to transform an individual's life yet we, as a people group, are impotent to influence our own nations? Do we not have one nation discipled? Forget discipling a nation – how about a sustained influence in a single city or town?
- Was Jesus seriously expecting nations to be taught when He told the disciples to go "make disciples of nations, teaching them all things I have taught you"? What are we missing?

What he finally discovered as his missing piece was the concept of micro churches within each Mountain. He found that when believers, even just two or three, within the same sphere of influence (be that a Mountain or a business or other entity in the Mountain) begin to meet and function together as the body of Christ, they force multiply their effectiveness.

"Force multiplier" is a military term. Per the US Department of Defense, it means: "A capability that, when added to and employed by a combat force, significantly increases the combat potential of that force and thus enhances the probability of successful mission accomplishment. (JP 3-05.1) (US DoD)"[24]

> *Once people begin to pray together rather than individually, their effectiveness increases exponentially.*

In other words, there is some factor that, when added, causes much greater effectiveness. Wikipedia explains the "multiplication factor" as, "The expected size increase required to have the same effectiveness without that advantage."[25] For example, if the new capability allows a group of fifty soldiers to accomplish what would require two hundred soldiers without it, the multiplication factor is four. Four times as many soldiers would have to be deployed to accomplish the same mission if that capability were not available.

In the case of believers beginning to work and pray together, Deuteronomy 32:30 tells us the multiplication factor is exponential. "How could one chase a thousand, And two put ten thousand to flight…?" When we are warring in the spirit realm, two can put to flight ten times as many as one alone. That is not simple multiplication. Once people begin to pray together rather than individually, their effectiveness increases exponentially. Wallnau sees the establishment of the micro churches and the force multiplier it provides as the key to waging effective warfare and displacing the demonic spirits controlling the sphere of influence. Once the demonic spirits are evicted, it becomes much easier for the Kingdom of God to manifest more fully.

In addition, those within the micro church can pray with each other, discerning where God wants them to be in their mountain and praying for the favor and opportunities for each to fulfill their God-given assignments. The prayers of those in the micro church can sometimes be much more effective because they understand the specifics of the jobs and roles and can target their prayers specifically. Often, our family or others who may be praying for us do not have that level of understanding about the work we do or know with whom we need favor for a particular issue. I liken it to a sniper using a high-powered rifle to take out a specific target versus a machine gun. The machine gun may make a lot of noise and mow down anything in its path, but it can leave a lot of collateral damage. Snipers can be much more effective, and they can often remain hidden and undetected. Of course, praying in the spirit in other tongues trumps any natural prayer. It is truly our secret weapon. Hopefully, that is being employed as well.

So far, I have only addressed the message as revealed to Loren Cunningham, Bill Bright, and Francis Schaeffer and then honed, illustrated, and taught by Lance Wallnau. Others who grasped this truth would follow, such as Michael Maiden who authored the previously referenced book, *Turn the World Upside Down: Discipling the Nations with the Seven Mountain Strategy*. There is another voice that God has been using to spread the Seven Mountain message since shortly after Lance Wallnau began teaching it. However, he did not get the message from Cunningham, Bright, Schaeffer, or Wallnau. The revelation was imparted directly to him by Holy Spirit. His journey is quite different from the journey of Lance Wallnau. While the basic message is the same, some of his revelation and applications are slightly different. Hence, you may need to shift gears a little as we move into his story.

Chapter 4

Same Revelation

Different Perspective

Many within the body of Christ were beginning to learn about the Seven Mountains and the need for believers to take their place in them from Lance Wallnau. Another segment in the body of Christ was hearing the same message from someone else. That was Johnny Enlow. Though he received the revelation differently, the underlying message is the same.

Referring to the quote at the beginning of Chapter 3, Johnny Enlow was a *theorist* as well as being a *researcher*, *teacher*, and *practitioner* of this message. He received the revelation, researched it, refined it, and has been teaching and practicing it since 2006. His wife, Elizabeth Enlow, has also worked beside him as a *researcher*, *teacher*, and *practitioner*. Per their website:

> Johnny Enlow is a social reformer, international speaker, and author of many books, including *The Seven Mountain Prophecy*, *The Seven Mountain Mantle*, *Rainbow God*, *The Seven Mountain Renaissance*, *Becoming A Superhero*, and *RISE*. He and his wife Elizabeth are passionately pursuing reformation of the 7 primary areas or mountains of culture as places that God desires to display the truth of His heart for the world – in Media, Arts and Entertainment, Government, Family, Religion, Economy, and Education. … They are co-founders of Restore7, which globally serves influencers in

> every area of society through the RISE Global Community and app.[26]

Like Loren Cunningham and Bill Bright, Johnny Enlow received the revelation about the Seven Mountains directly from God. His story and his journey to get to the point of understanding, teaching, and implementing this concept were vastly different. Since he was the theorist (receiver of the revelation) and receiving the revelation was a process for Enlow, it will take a bit longer to tell his story.

The Early Years

While Lance Wallnau was growing up in Pennsylvania in an affluent setting, Johnny Enlow was growing up in the jungles of Peru surrounded by poverty. At the time, Peru was listed at 90 percent *extreme* poverty, meaning 90 percent of the population made less than one dollar a day. That remained true well into this century and becomes part of the story. Enlow was born in Lima, Peru, to American missionaries who spent more than fifty years ministering to the people of Peru while rearing their eight children there. His parents were spirit-filled and witnessed not only salvations, but healings and miracles in their ministry. Those days instilled two things in the young Enlow from which he still draws: 1) learning to trust and obey God's direction and 2) seeing God's Spirit move in signs and wonders, healings, and miracles.

In his early years, he was introduced to the concept of present-day apostles and prophets, filled with the Spirit at the age of eight, and learned about casting out demons and spiritual warfare. His faith walk continued to grow and seeing healings and other miracles remained "normal Christianity" for him. He expected it. He also learned in his youth to hear God speaking to him, personally.

In his early teens, he became like the Bereans in that he "searched the Scriptures daily to find out whether these things were so" (Acts

17:11), especially related to doctrinal issues. That led to what he calls "a defining moment" in his life at age fourteen. He made a decision to trust what he believed Holy Spirit was saying to him and what he read in the Word over anyone else's opinion or doctrine.[27] This standard of listening to Holy Spirit and searching the Word would anchor the rest of his life. It was his ability to hear the Holy Spirit and then search out what He is saying in scripture that enabled Enlow to receive the Seven Mountain revelation as he did.

At eighteen, he moved to the United States, became a painter, and eventually owned his own painting business. He continued to study the Word of God deeply, even though the two things he said he would never do were to pastor a church or be a missionary. He had lived through enough of that! So, like Wallnau, he did not choose to go into vocational ministry.

Answering the Call

In January 1995, the Toronto Blessing "broke out," as we say, and Enlow went. There he witnessed an intensity of the presence and power of God that was new to him. He was very accustomed to seeing people saved, healed, delivered, and even seeing miracles. He was not used to the sudden "ramp up," as he called it, of God's presence and power he saw demonstrated. It was there he surrendered to the call on his life, telling God, "If You will accompany me with this kind of presence and this kind of power, I will go to the nations."[28]

Enlow believed taking the kind of presence and power of God he was seeing and experiencing in Toronto to the nations would change them; it would change their societal structures. He knew that God did not just want to save and heal people; He wanted to make life better for them in every way. ("I have come that they may have life, and that they may have it more abundantly," John 10:10.) God did not just want to save souls; He wanted to transform lives. That was the thing for which he had been crying out. He had wanted to see nations changed for the sake of their people. *He wanted to see the transformation of cities and nations.*

Enlow immediately began reaching out to ministry connections in Peru, wanting to take this transforming power to a people and a nation that he loved and knew desperately needed it (and to which he was called). Thus, Johnny Enlow entered the ministry as a short-term missionary while still running his painting business. He would go on to become a church planter and pastor and eventually be recognized as the prophet and teacher that he is.

Enlow believed taking the kind of presence and power of God he was seeing and experiencing in Toronto to the nations would change them; it would change their societal structures.

He started taking small ministry teams to Peru in 1995. He would preach a short message and then simply invite the Holy Spirit to come. (For those not familiar with the Vineyard movement led by John Wimber, "Come, Holy Spirit," was a frequent request in Vineyard services, including in Toronto.) As God had promised him in Toronto, when Enlow invited Holy Spirit to come, He came with His presence and with the power to save, heal, deliver, and work miracles. The blind, the deaf, those severely crippled, and many more were healed. These things happened again and again, in meeting after meeting, whether he was the one praying or it was someone on his team. Over the next few years, thousands were saved, healed, and delivered.[29]

Yet, he became frustrated because when he would go back a year or two later, there was no noticeable change. There was no visible change in the poverty level, the crime rate, the school systems, or other areas of their daily lives. He answered the call of God to the nations because he believed the power of God he had seen in Toronto would change not just people but their living conditions. But, when he returned, he did not see that change. How could so many people be saved and touched so deeply by God, yet there be no visible transformation? Why were blessings not sustained? Some people had even lost their physical healing.

"How do we see the cities (and nations) transformed?"

This became so frustrating to him that he began to wrestle with God over the issue. He asked God questions like, "How do we affect the economy? How do we affect education? How do we affect employment numbers? How do we affect the crime rate?" He could see things that needed to be improved, but he did not know how to improve them. He recounts going through "years of simultaneous frustration and of testifying of what God was doing," seeing Him heal people with creative miracles. But where was the lasting change?[30]

Enlow and Wallnau had wrestled with the same issue. Both were asking the same question: "How do we see the cities (and nations) transformed?"

Often to get a new revelation, we must first become dissatisfied with where we are. It is that dissatisfaction or, as Enlow called it, frustration which drives us to press in for something different – a new way of seeing the situation, a different way of responding, or a new revelation. However, until we have that new direction, we must stay our course. We should not stop doing what we know to do; rather we should remain faithful in our current assignment until we get a change in direction from God. We must keep our hand on the plow and keep looking forward. (See Luke 9:62.) Enlow continued to go and minister and see people saved and healed and rejoiced in that. But he continued to wrestle with God for the key to seeing the lasting change that affected not just individuals but structures that would change cities, regions, and nations.

Moving to the Next Level

In 1999, Enlow's ministry was taken to a new level. God gave him a new instruction saying, "I want you to begin to reach the 'up and outers.'"[31] Enlow initially resisted, not at all being comfortable with "up and outers" (whoever they were). Unlike Wallnau who had become accustomed to dealing with business executives and leaders in his secular career, Enlow was accustomed to ministering primarily to the poor and downcast as his parents had done. God made His point clear by adding, "I'm not asking you; I'm telling you." God directed him to begin to meet with the mayors of the cities in which he ministered.[32]

Holy Spirit prophetically revealed seven major discoveries that would turn their economy around.

Let me summarize a very long story.

His next ministry trip was to be to Saposoa, Peru. Saposoa was so crime ridden that his ministry friends in Peru strongly advised him not to go there. The crime caused it to be very economically depressed; it was an extremely poor area. He went ahead with the ministry trip and arranged for a meeting with the mayor. The mayor was new to his position and genuinely concerned about the welfare of the people. To Enlow's surprise, during that meeting Holy Spirit prophetically revealed seven *major* discoveries that would be made in the area that would turn their economy around. The discoveries revealed prophetically were: two salt mines, a zinc mine, a silver mine, a touristic waterfall, a touristic thermal spring, and (just for good measure) a lost city of the Incas.[33] Even Enlow was astounded at what he had seen … and prophesied! When the images identifying the things to be discovered stopped coming, Enlow heard the Lord add: "I'm telling you all these things so that when they happen, … you recognize … *these are because God is good.* He's looking out for your city, and He's looking out for you and wants to help you." [34] (Emphasis added.)

Johnny Enlow had encountered the goodness of God in a new way, on a whole new level, that day. Without sharing the gospel or any offer of salvation with the mayor (who was Catholic but not yet born again), God had made some astounding promises for the prosperity of the region. On that same trip, he noticed a marked increase in the number of salvations, healings, and miracles in their meetings. Obedience always yields blessing, and God was demonstrating His goodness.

For Enlow, it was the Biblical reality that nations should be walking to the light of the sons of God that he could not reconcile.

Over the next eighteen months, *everything prophesied happened.* All seven sites prophesied were discovered.[35] The mayor informed him that everything he had said had come to pass and gave him permission to do whatever he wanted to do in the city. On his next trip, the team held meetings in Central Square for several evenings with an overwhelming number of salvations and physical healings.[36] This was a novel approach to evangelism. It started with promising help from a good God and then watching the goodness of God lead the people to repentance.

Word spread and Enlow and his teams began ministering in other areas of Peru (and in other Latin American countries) with similar experiences and results. Many people would be saved, healed, and delivered in their meetings, and God would speak to the leaders of things that would shift their economies. At the same time Enlow was rejoicing in all that he was seeing God do both in individuals and in the economy of cities and regions, he was continuing to wrestle with God. He still was not seeing the overall transformation he knew should happen. The societal structures were not being changed. To put it in terms he did not yet understand, people were being touched in the Mountain of Religion, economies were being transformed in the Mountain of Economy, but the other five Mountains were not being impacted. Hence, society as a whole was not being transformed.

For Enlow, it was the Biblical reality that *nations should be walking to the light of the sons of God* that he could not reconcile. How did that happen? It had been frustrating him for years. He pressed God:

> Lord, in Isaiah 60:3, You say nations will walk to the light of the sons of God. That's different than souls getting saved. How are we going to see nations walk to the light of the sons of God unless the *systems* of that nation are affected as well?[37] (Emphasis added.)

The more his faith grew by seeing what all God was doing, including all the salvations, healings, and miracles, the more he wanted to see Him move beyond individuals and churches. He longed to see God move in cities and nations, transforming not just their economy but all their societal structures. He longed to see so much of the Kingdom of God show up in such a way that you could see it in the statistics reported by the city. He was looking for changes in such things as the economic measures, crime rates, and education scores.[38] He was seeking *transformation of the city*, and not just salvation of the people in it.

The Seven Mountain Revelation

"Suddenly," after years of frustration and wrestling with God, in August 2006, Johnny Enlow encountered what he describes as a "big shift." (Do you not love God's "suddenlies"? They usually come after *years* of prayer and perseverance!) At this point, he and Elizabeth had planted and were pastoring a church in Atlanta, Georgia. Cal Pierce, from The Healing Rooms, was conducting a conference for them. He gave Enlow a prophetic word that said, "Johnny, the Lord says, 'Get ready, get ready. I'm about to show you what you've been asking Me. I'm going to show you how My Kingdom is coming.'"[39] Enlow recounts his "big shift" this way:

> Almost immediately, within a few days, it started with some kind of dream encounter with the Lord is all that I can call it. Half dream, half encounter. The word of the Lord did come and say, "I'm going to show you what you have been asking for; *I'm going to show you how My Kingdom can reach all areas of society.*"
>
> So, He began to show me a new template for this. What we would now call the Seven Mountain Mandate would be the template. I hadn't heard anyone else talk about the Seven Mountains at this time at all. He didn't use the terminology Seven Mountains in the first conversation.
>
> He said, "In the same way the children of Israel had to go into the promised land and there were seven enemy nations greater and mightier than them …" out of Deuteronomy. (Deuteronomy 7 talks about the Hittites, the Jebusites, the Girgashites, all the "ites," seven "ites" – and it says, "seven nations greater and mightier than them.") … He said, "In that same way, where *My people are called to occupy with My presence, to bring who I am, My solutions, My Kingdom*, to these areas where the enemy presently is."
>
> There was a quick understanding that, for instance, the Hittites had to do with the Mountain of Media. Their name means fear and terror. He says, "The enemy, the way he assaults that Mountain is through releasing fear, terror, bad news, worse news, gossip. *My Kingdom comes in the opposite spirit.*"
>
> It was a progressive, night by night, revealing. I think two, three, four hours a night awake getting more and more

> revelation from Him. The revelation would often instruct me to study this, to look at this scripture, to look this up. Out of it came my first book on the Seven Mountains that was released in English in January of 2008, *The Seven Mountain Prophecy: Unveiling the Coming Elijah Revolution.*[40]
>
> (Emphasis added.)

This was the revelation, the new template he had been seeking. It was new to him, and to most in the body of Christ, that the Kingdom of God is intended to show up in each of these Mountains, not just in our churches in the Mountain of Religion. The objective is not just to have good church meetings and to see many people get saved and healed "but that *the Kingdom of God is revealed* in each of the seven primary spheres of society."[41] (Emphasis added.) Just touching the Mountain of Religion and the Mountain of Economy was not enough. All areas of society need to be reached. In doing so, we would have to "drive out the ites" from each of these areas (deal with the principality controlling each one). Then the opposite spirit of the Kingdom of God could be released more fully into each. Enlow continued: "What came out of that, I began calling it spheres – or mountains. The Lord connected it to Isaiah 2:2, 'in the last days, the mountain of the house of the Lord will be exalted in the tops of the mountains.' I liked that language as well."[42]

The seven areas he identified were:

- Media
- Education
- Government
- Economy
- Family
- Arts & Entertainment
- Religion

It is amazing how Holy Spirit can convey the same information to different vessels, yet it remains consistent. If the message is not consistent, it is not that Holy Spirit did not convey the same information; the issue of conflicting revelations is a problem in hearing or interpreting.

Enlow had known for years that to change living conditions in a way that truly improved the lives of the people, it was not just a matter of getting enough people saved, healed, and delivered. Tremendous economic breakthroughs precipitated by God releasing prophetic words, watching over them, and guiding individuals to bring them to pass had begun in 1999 and 2000. Yet, these areas were not being changed in a sustainable, transformative way. He knew this new revelation of infiltrating *every* realm of society with the Kingdom of God was what would finally bring true transformation. He received and began teaching this message in 2006.

To quickly finish the testimony of Peru, let me provide some statistics of what God has done. Remember that Enlow received and began preaching the Seven Mountain message in 2006. This message was added to the hidden treasures God was revealing prophetically all over the nation and was very much a part of what happened. It is still having its effects in Peru and other Latin American countries. Statistically, Peru went from 90 percent *extreme poverty* in 2000 to 2.4 percent *poverty* in 2018.* It had moved from being tied with Haiti for the poorest nation in Latin America economically to leading the continent; what occurred became referred to globally as the "Peruvian Economic Miracle."[43] Lima, a city of ten million people, went from 50 percent unemployment to 9 percent (and then even lower).[44] One of the best results was that the church in Peru doubled between 2010 and 2018 – without any "revival" as we would understand it. It grew because people recognized the goodness of God.[45] This was the

---

* This was the last year for which statistics were available when the information was compiled.

impact of coupling the Seven Mountain message with prophetic words revealing God's goodness through resources He had provided that had heretofore remained hidden.

Johnny Enlow now knows the Seven Mountain revelation had been received and taught by others before he received it; he just did not know that at the time. He knows *he* received the message by revelation from the Holy Spirit through a series of nightly encounters and then searching the Word. It was a revelation he had been seeking for years and one which was supernaturally revealed to him. He did not know that it had been revealed to others until after he began teaching it.[46]

Once he began teaching it, Enlow began to see God's power demonstrated at even higher levels. In the early days of teaching this message, significant signs often manifested when he would begin to teach this new revelation in a new geographical area. He quickly realized that if the body of Christ really grasped and began living this, it would change not only cities but nations. The Peruvian Economic Miracle was the first fruits.

Comparisons

Bill Bright and Loren Cunningham were each seeking the key to how to *disciple nations*. Johnny Enlow and Lance Wallnau were each seeking the key to *transforming cities and nations*. Yet the answer was the same. If you *disciple* the city, region, or nation (teaching them the principles of the Kingdom as Jesus taught), it will become *transformed*, just as individuals are transformed when discipled.

For Enlow, the starting point of the revelation was going into the Mountains and driving the ruling principalities out so that the expression of the Kingdom of God could be released in its place. Just as he had received the revelation of associating one of the enemy nations listed in Deuteronomy 7 to each of the Mountains, he was shown the principality ruling over each one. (He was also shown other aspects* for each Mountain, including strategies for each. For more information on the other aspects, see *RISE: A Reformer's Handbook for the Seven Mountains*.[47])

No matter how much blessing God releases, as He had done in Peru, unless the thieves (principalities) are removed, the people will not prosper long term. For example, most of the wealth from one of the gold mines discovered as a fulfillment to one of the prophecies was lost due to corruption. For real transformation to occur in a city or nation, the "ites" must be driven out of all the systems or spheres of influence. Then the systems can be shifted to operate out of Kingdom principles and His blessings be sustained. (After the corruption was addressed, an even larger gold mine was discovered. That demonstrates God's goodness and His redemption.)

Likewise, Lance Wallnau realized the need to deal with the demonic powers as he had done as a consultant in large corporations. His revelation of the micro churches being established in each Mountain (or business or other entity within the Mountain) is a strategy to get the spiritual strength needed to first deal with the demonic forces. Then the micro churches can more effectively advance the Kingdom and its influence within that Mountain, at whatever location in the Mountain that micro church has influence and spiritual authority.

Now that we have explored how both men came to be teaching on the Seven Mountains, let us focus on the message itself. In the next chapter, we will look at each of the Mountains individually.

---

* While Johnny Enlow's Seven Mountain revelation includes several additional aspects, this comparison will only address the commonality. The other aspects provide a more complete message and deserve study.

Chapter 5
The Seven Mountains Explained

Over time, a consistent list of the Seven Mountains has emerged (though, as previously discussed, there are some who have started to vary the categories). Unfortunately, what has not emerged are definitive definitions for each Mountain. In part, the titles make them self-explanatory. However, questions often arise when one starts studying these in detail. For example, "Where is healthcare?" "Where is science & technology?" To bring clarity to the dividing lines, I will discuss each one briefly.

For a more in-depth dive on each Mountain, Johnny Enlow devotes an entire chapter to each Mountain in *The Seven Mountain Prophecy*.[48] He and Elizabeth Enlow do the same in both *Rainbow God*[49] and *RISE: A Reformer's Handbook for the Seven Mountains*[50] (hereafter referred to as "*RISE*"). Michael Maiden does the same in *Turn the World Upside Down: Discipling the Nations with the Seven Mountain Strategy*[51] referenced in Chapter 3.

Media

Media includes much more today than it did in past generations. Some of us remember the days when there were two primary sources for news – the news on one of three television networks (ABC, CBS, or NBC) and the daily local newspaper. The television networks usually had thirty minutes of local news, which included the local weather in the morning, midday, and late night. In the early evening, the broadcast would include thirty minutes of national news in addition to the local news and weather. In most places, the newspaper was printed and distributed once a day; some larger cities had a morning and an evening edition. National news magazines were published monthly, and a few local radio stations might have five minutes of news at the top of the hour or a half-hour segment twice a day.

Today, with the plethora of television networks that broadcast news twenty-four hours a day, not only to traditional platforms (television or "cable") but to multiple streaming services, we are in a "news on demand" culture. One no longer must be in front of their television set at a specific time to watch the news. Weather forecasts are also available at any time for any location. Newspapers and magazines now must maintain an online presence with constant updates, even if they do still publish a physical version.

Add to those changes all the podcasters that fill the various streaming services such as YouTube, Rumble, Substack, Instagram, and TikTok. In large part, where someone chooses to post is driven by the type of content and the desired audience. Many post to multiple sites. Even the sites that were initially designed as social media, such as Facebook and X (originally Twitter), now have news outlets and commentators of all types posting to them. Today's issue is not trying to get news; it is determining which news sources one wants to get (or one believes they can trust). The cover for the May 2025 edition of *Newsmax* magazine featured a graphic with the text "BIG MEDIA MELTDOWN." In the article, they quoted an October 2024 Gallup survey that reported: "only 31% of Americans expressed 'a great deal'

Today's issue is not trying to get news; it is determining which news sources one wants to get (or one believes they can trust).

or 'a fair amount' of confidence in the media's ability to report news fully, accurately, and fairly."[52]

The total inundation of information has made Media one of the top molders of culture. Lance Wallnau often credits William Wilberforce with the statement, "A nation is shaped through a sustained pattern of public persuasion."[53] To show its timelessness, this same statement has been credited to Abraham Lincoln and was often used by American political scientist and former Director of Virginia Tech's Department of Communication, Robert E. Denton, Jr. Today, we have the phenomenon that different major news networks use the same talking points with the same wording. A phrase is coined, or key talking points are developed and distributed to numerous networks of like ideology. You can switch between them and hear the same exact phrases in broadcast segment after broadcast segment.

The Fairness Doctrine was mandated by the Federal Communications Commission (FCC) in 1949. It "required licensed radio and television broadcasters to present fair and balanced coverage of controversial issues of interest to their communities."[54] This regulation mandated that "Individuals who were the subject of editorials or who perceived themselves to be the subject of unfair attacks in news programming were to be granted an opportunity to reply"[55] at a similar time of coverage. (E.g., if the news piece was originally broadcast in prime time, the response must be aired in prime time.) This mandate was lifted by the FCC in 1987 when it was challenged as a violation of free speech.

Alarmingly, not only have we seen a drastic increase in biased or "unfair attacks in news programming," but the content is no longer required to have any basis in fact; it can be entirely fabricated. Yet, when people hear it multiple times from multiple sources, they believe it to be true. Their opinion is "shaped through a sustained pattern of public persuasion." It still works! Unfortunately, it is currently being used primarily for evil rather than good.

The good news is that in the past decade or so, there have been many fresh news sources springing up with the goal of bringing integrity back to both reporting and commentary. In addition to the plethora of online podcasters, there are brand-new news outlets that publish online and email out updates daily or multiple times a day. There are also new networks broadcasting on cable television and on various streaming platforms. One example is *The Epoch Times*, established in 2000 as a weekly, printed newspaper with a digital presence that is constantly updated. It recently added Epoch TV. Their byline is "Truth, Tradition, Hope." In *RISE*, the Enlows explain, "Media that blesses presents truth through a hopeful perspective that gives the listener the ability to envision a happy ending, even when it is news that is difficult to hear."[56] *The Epoch Times* embodies what the Enlows were saying about presenting "truth through a hopeful perspective."

Let us pray that the restoration of truth and accuracy is a trend that continues. It requires having truthful and honest reporters and management. We need more with the core values of honesty and integrity to flood this Mountain as truth speakers who bring hope. Traditionally, the only sources offering hope on their news were channels owned by Christian organizations such as CBN News or Victory News. There are new sources arising, independent of any specific Christian organization, yet carrying Kingdom values. In *The Seven Mountain Prophecy*, Johnny Enlow points out, "There is a difference between seeing yourself as a journalist who happens to be a Christian, and a son or daughter of the King on a specific assignment."[57] We need more King's kids who know their assignment – whether to the Mountain of Media or elsewhere. There is a shift occurring in the Media Mountain. May it accelerate!

Family

The Family Mountain may appear to be straightforward. As Wallnau often puts it, "You and your house,"[58] and, of course, grandma and other extended family. But it includes anything that affects the healthy functioning of "you and your house." It includes the medical field, counseling and mental health services, and social services for families or individuals (children or adults). In one sense, this is everyone's Mountain, even when we do not work in it. When it is not a healthy environment, it affects how well we function as an individual in any of the other Mountains to which we are called.

We need those called and gifted in these fields to bring breakthroughs in the areas of medicine, health, and overall wholeness.

It is easy to look around in the US today and see dysfunctional families – or dysfunctional people within a family. There are, of course, the long-standing problems of alcohol, drugs, verbal and physical abuse, pornography, adultery, and divorce within families. Today, families sometimes face issues with a child who has become convinced (usually by someone outside the family) that they have gender identity issues. The growing number of those identifying as LGBTQ+ is an issue that affects the Family Mountain. Add the issue of human trafficking of both children and adults, with teens and even pre-teens being groomed online. They can be lured into a situation in which they become victims or even captives. As the Enlows identify in *RISE*, a spirit of perversion is the principality that seeks to control this Mountain, often partnering with the spirit of rejection.[59] It has had control of too many individuals in this Mountain for too long. For traffickers, perversion is joined by greed (the principality identified as ruling the Business Mountain[60]) because selling perversion has become their business.

There is much that needs to be done in this Mountain. Returning to where most families consist of a father and mother who love each other, stay married, and raise their children in a loving and respectful environment would be a great start. Medical and child services need to be working with families towards the mental and physical well-being of children, rather than indoctrination and exploitation. We need those called and gifted in these fields to bring breakthroughs in the areas of medicine, health, and overall wholeness. The Church plays a critical role in getting the Family Mountain back on track. Part of that role is sending people who are called to work in medicine, psychology, social services, or similar areas into their mission field to bring the influence of the Kingdom with its solutions and its change.

Arts & Entertainment / Celebration

Celebration seems to fit this Mountain best in that it covers so many different areas, though these areas can be categorized as the Entertainment portion of Arts & Entertainment. Hence, either term works. This Mountain includes all forms of art from what we typically call “artwork” (such as paintings or drawings) to musical artists, performers, and athletes. It also includes celebration events.

One thing that can make understanding the Mountains confusing is how they seem to overlap. For example, is the celebration of a high school or college graduation in this Mountain, or is it in the Education Mountain? Or is it in the Family Mountain? It would seem logical that the actual ceremony is part of what the Education Mountain provides. The graduation party thrown by parents would be in the Family Mountain. The graduates going out for an evening of celebration with their peers would fall here on the Mountain of Celebration.

In his "Endgame: A Time for Peace and a Time for War" teaching series, Lance Wallnau states that Entertainment is "the suspension of reality."[61] It should be the opposite of Media, which he had previously said, "should be a disclosure of reality" and is "to be telling the people the truth."[62] He continues, "Entertainment is the discipling force."[63] To Wallnau's point, we do not have to look far to see that most of the discipling that has been done through Entertainment over the past few decades has not been advancing the Kingdom of God; rather it has been advancing the kingdom of darkness.

Influence is the key.

Both young people and adults have been simultaneously intrigued with and desensitized to the world of the occult and other evil through Arts & Entertainment. This has occurred through shows like *Buffy the Vampire Slayer* (the movie and television series) and *Harry Potter* (in books, movies, and a theme park) and a plentitude of horror movies. Most people have no idea of the doors they open to the demonic realm by watching shows of this nature and would not believe it if someone tried to tell them. It did not start with these. It started much more subtly with shows like *Bewitched* which aired on prime-time television from 1964 until 1972. It was another twenty years before *Buffy* hit the big screen. The water in the proverbial pot was cold when we frogs were placed in it.

We have Christian movies, television networks and shows, music, and art. These are subcultures that service almost exclusively Christians and are, therefore, in the Religion Mountain, not in the Arts & Entertainment Mountain. What is needed are people with Kingdom principles working in this Mountain in secular television, movies, and music, producing wholesome, yet cutting-edge and entertaining products. God is *the Creator*. He is not short on imagination. He needs people through whom to work. We are beginning to see this. It needs to increase, which means we need more righteous people stepping into these roles.

This trend is spreading within the movie industry. Actors and actresses are pulling away from companies that are promoting immoral agendas (such as LGBTQ+) for those that are producing morally clean films which promote family values. Many of these are very vocal about their faith. One example has been a movement of actors and actresses from the Hallmark networks to the newer Great American Family (GAF) network because of Hallmark's move toward wokeness and GAF's commitment to family values.[64] As with the new news broadcasting agencies returning to honesty and integrity in reporting, there are many new movie production companies arising with traditional values. GAF is just one example. This does not mean all their content has a Christian theme but that it is something to which you can take your family without having to preview it first. The biggest inroad at this point seems to be in sports, with a growing number of athletes, coaches, and team owners being vocal about their faith. More importantly, they are influencing those around them daily. *Influence is the key.*

Economy / Business

The term Economy implies a larger sphere than Business. I would argue that there is business conducted in every Mountain, even the Religion Mountain. It is not just that some churches or other religious institutions operate like businesses these days. There are businesses that support the Mountain of Religion. For example, a Christian publishing company or a Christian bookstore exists solely for the purpose of supporting the Religion Mountain. The same is true in any of the other Mountains. A movie theater would reside in the Arts & Entertainment Mountain. A military defense contractor would be in the Government Mountain. A doctor's office or clinic would be in the Family Mountain. And so forth.

The term Economy is more wide-reaching. It deals with the overall flow of resources. Merriam-Webster Unabridged online dictionary defines *economy* as: "the structure of economic life in a country or area : an economic system."[65] It is always interesting when another form of the word is used to define the word. Their definition for *economic* includes: "of, relating to, or concerned with the production, distribution, and consumption of commodities." A secondary definition is: "operated or produced on a profitable basis : producing an excess of returns over expenditures."[66] These get us a little closer to the point.

Production includes the research and development needed before a product can be produced, which includes science and technology. (Hence, my belief that science and technology should remain part of this Mountain.) Products must be produced and distributed. Not only is there the issue of distributing the product, but there is also the issue of receiving the materials needed to produce it, which is, in turn, another company's distribution of their product. This chain of events is called the supply chain. We all became familiar with that term during 2020 and 2021 when we saw pictures of ships with anchors dropped off the coast. They were waiting for their turn to dock and unload the supplies that were missing from the store shelves or the parts or materials needed to build them. Consumption includes getting the product to the person or entity (e.g., a business) that wants it. There is, of course, sales and marketing that go into identifying those consumers.

Having worked in the manufacturing sector, this is all quite familiar to me. However, it works for any sector. Services are also produced and consumed. They may have to be distributed (e.g., if an attorney draws up a power of attorney for someone, it must be "distributed" to the person it empowers to be of use, if needed). Or they may be distributed as part of the production (e.g., a hair stylist delivers the product by performing the service on the individual who comes to them). The key to a healthy economy is in the second part of the definition above: "operated or produced on a profitable basis."

> *Production includes the research and development needed before a product can be produced, which includes science and technology.*

Currently, there is a lot of talk about the global economy. It is, of course, affected by the economies of the individual nations. Many would prefer to stay blissfully ignorant of how it works, but that does not prevent it from affecting their pocketbook or retirement investments. Of course, there is a need for Kingdom-minded people within any business. More so, we need them in the positions of those whose decisions affect the economies of cities, states, and nations. Shifts in these economies affect us all. We need people there who are seeking the good of society and not their own good or the good of the controlling group to which they belong or for which they work. These men and women need wisdom that can only come from God. He is the only One who can *always* accurately predict the future!

Religion

Some refer to the Religion Mountain as the Church Mountain. It is broader than just Christianity; it covers all religions. In fairness, the people listening to this teaching or reading about this message are probably Christian and, at this point, most likely of a Pentecostal or charismatic persuasion. From a Christian perspective, Michael Maiden hit the mark in defining "The Purpose of the Church." He states:

> The Church is ordained to reach the lost and then train Christians in the truth, power, and dynamics of God's Kingdom. It is to equip followers of Christ to return to (or find) their places of influence in the seven mountains of culture to do their part in bringing God's Kingdom to earth.[67]

Unfortunately, as a whole, the Church has *not* been hitting that mark. The gospel of salvation is still the focus for most churches, denominations, and believers rather than the gospel of the Kingdom. Until it is understood that we are here, on earth, to bring the influence of the Kingdom of God to earth, there is no grid on which to place this message of going into the various Mountains to bring the influence of the Kingdom to them.

Today, Socialism, Marxism, and Communism have very well-defined playbooks of how to get imbedded in each of the Mountains.

There are other groups that well understand the need to go into each of these spheres to be able to influence them with their beliefs. They also understand the need to work together across spheres to effect the change they want to see in the culture. And they have been doing it. Islam understands and implements this. We have experienced a measure of that in the United States; they have gotten even more of a foothold in Canada and Great Britain. According to BillionBibles.org, "Sharia law in the United States of America has reached penetration phase 3."[68] Phase 3 (of 5) is "Infiltration." Its description begins with, "When Muslims gain critical mass in a few cities, they begin to infiltrate key institutions of the host society."[69] Those institutions are the Mountains. To see how much ground they have gained, look under the "Sharia Law" tab on the BillionBibles.org website. It will probably surprise and alarm you.

There are ideologies such as Socialism and Marxism (the goal of which is to move a society to Communism without the use of military force) that are extremely familiar with these steps as well. These may not be technically classified as religions, but I propose they function as such. They seek to replace anything that exists that would hold the allegiance of the people rather than the government or the regime in charge. Often, their leaders expect the literal worship of the people.

On May 1, 2025, Rod D. Martin posted an article on Substack titled "May Day," with the subtitle "Socialism is a religion. This is its high holy day." In it, he points out that Karl Marx never developed a plan; it was developed years later by others. Marx simply outlined his ten points in the *Communist Manifesto,* which he coauthored with Friedrich Engels. Martin maintains, "[Marx] never defined them further. He never saw a need. Marx had grander work in mind. *He was producing a religion.*"[70] (Emphasis added.)

Marx's philosophy might have died with him had it not been for others who picked it up and refined it, eventually developing strategy and the detailed playbooks to execute it. Today, Socialism, Marxism, and Communism have very well-defined playbooks of how to get imbedded in each of the Mountains. A look at history shows they have executed on this plan over and over in country after country.

> *While the Church in America was sleeping, those subscribing to Socialism and Marxism have been disciplining our nation for decades.*

Once in power, suppressing other religions, particularly Judaism and Christianity, is one of the first things they go after, knowing that these belief systems are their greatest threat. At times, they even frame their political opponents as being a "cult," a term usually associated with religion. The term is being used more and more frequently to brand those with differing ideological or political beliefs, even though they do not fit the definition. It is part of the propaganda war that is key component of their playbook. It has become increasingly obvious that the goal of many so-called "Progressives" is Socialism or Marxism with the ultimate intent to move the US toward yielding her sovereignty to a globalist agenda and leader and stripping her citizens of their God-given freedoms. That is *not* the direction in which most Americans want to progress! (Can you spell "one world government"?)

While the Church in America was sleeping, those subscribing to Socialism and Marxism have been disciplining our nation for decades. We are now faced with the task of "deprogramming" (to use the cult analogy) those who have succumbed to that message. Many of them (by design in their playbook) have no understanding of where it is leading or the full intent of those promoting it. If they knew the intended destination, most would not have chosen to join. Deception is a major portion of the strategy.

Fortunately, our deprogramming methodology is to simply bring them truth and pray that their eyes will be opened and their ears will be unstopped so they can see and hear and be set free. Light will always dispel darkness. This clearly shows why the Church must wake up and get involved. It also explains why those opposing the gospel of the Kingdom do not want us to get involved and will always seek to silence our voice.

While all the spheres touch each other to an extent, the Mountain of Religion and, specifically, the Church, should be touching all the other Mountains. We will look at this in more detail in Section 2. For now, I will again reference the quote from Michael Maiden. The Church *must* be training believers to find their place in one or more of the Mountains and bring the influence of the Kingdom of God to it. That is the message of the Seven Mountain Mandate. That is how we disciple nations.

We need to go into the "world" (each Mountain) and do as the Romans did when they entered a fresh territory. They brought the customs of Rome and transitioned the people in that territory to begin to look, act, sound, and think like a Roman in every way (e.g., language, food, clothing, architecture, money, and laws). That is what Islam does. That is also what Socialism, Marxism, and Communism all drive toward. They cry "separation of church and state" (which is *not* in nor implied by our Constitution) when Christians try to bring their values to bear in any of the Mountains except within the Church.

All the while, they know that is *exactly* what they have been doing and intend to keep doing. Luke 16:8 tells us that "the sons of this world are more shrewd in their generation than the sons of light." The Greek word translated "shrewd" is "phronimos"[71] and means: "intelligent, wise; prudent, i.e., mindful of one's interests."[72] We need to get shrewd! The Church must learn how to train and deploy believers into society.

The Church must learn how to train and deploy believers into society.

Additionally, we in the Church must make ourselves aware of what is happening in each of the other Mountains. When there are issues that are driving something in one of the other Mountains in a way that is contrary to the Kingdom of God, the Church must not only speak up but take action. (Even William Pitt, who did not profess to be a Christian, realized that as he sought to convince William Wilberforce to remain in parliament.) Our nation slid into the state in which we now find it because the silent majority remained silent and did nothing. There has always been a remnant who understood and fought with all they had. Until recently, the remnant has been small. Many more are now awake and have joined it. We cannot allow them to go back to sleep. Once territory is gained (or re-gained), we must continue to occupy it. Per Merriam-Webster's, one of the definitions for "occupy" is "to hold possession of."[73] It does no good to take ground if it is not held.

There are other institutions or efforts in the Mountain of Religion besides churches, temples, and synagogues. As mentioned in the discussion for the Economy / Business Mountain, there are businesses that exist for the sole purpose of servicing churches or para-church ministries. These belong in this Mountain. Similarly, Christian radio, television, magazines, podcasts, and the like, are a sub-culture to the Media Mountain as Christian music, movies, art, and such are to the Mountain of Arts & Entertainment. These subcultures belong here.

Bible Colleges or Seminaries whose sole purpose is Biblical studies belong here. Conversely, a school that is accredited to teach the standard curriculum and issue state-accepted diplomas would be in the Education Mountain, even though it is owned, operated, and staffed by Christians and teaches Bible courses.

Education

The Education Mountain might be the most easily understood. It is the sphere in which people are taught or trained. That can be through the public education system, a private school, a Christian school (that meets the required education standards), or home-schooling. It includes everything from pre-K through graduate school at a college or university. (Day care centers are in the Family Mountain.) It includes technical training schools for such things as auto mechanics, plumbing, or specialized skills for factory work and specialized schools like a culinary school or a school for cosmetology. It is any school or organization that provides a standardized educational or training program. However, as previously stated, a Bible College or Seminary that only teaches Biblical studies and related topics (such as hermeneutics) would be in the Religion Mountain.

"God does not hold the state or federal government accountable for how our children are educated; He considers the family to have the first place of responsibility and then the church."

This Mountain contains not just the teachers but administrators, principals and deans, school superintendents, school board members, and more. It contains all who are making decisions about the educational content and educational process. This includes those determining the required curriculum and the books to be used to teach it. This is usually at a state level. Too much has been at the federal level with the Department of Education, established in 1977 by President Jimmy Carter. President Donald Trump's administration is working to dismantle it, with those decision rights being returned to the state level where they belong constitutionally. This makes having the right people in place to make those decisions at the state and local levels even more important because those people will once again have control.

Quoting again from Michael Maiden:

> God does not hold the state or federal government accountable for how our children are educated; He considers the family to have the first place of responsibility and then the church.
>
> *[You] train up a child in the way he should go [and in keeping with his individual gift or bent], and when he is old he will not depart from it (Proverbs 22:6 AMP).*[74]

Regardless of whom is chosen to educate one's children, the basic responsibility to "train" them "in the way [they] should go" is squarely placed on the parents and within the Family Mountain. This is not talking about teaching them algebra, biology, or how to diagram a sentence. It speaks to core values and principles that should be instilled in them based on the Word of God. That responsibility cannot be relegated to someone else, even if the child is attending a Christian school. What is being taught in Sunday School, Children's Church, and mid-week events for children or youth at your local church should re-enforce and augment what is being taught at home. If a child grows into adulthood without those core values, it is not the fault of the school or church they attended. That responsibility lies squarely with the parents or guardian, the ones with responsibility for their care.

Government

The Government Mountain is broad. It includes all branches of government – for the United States, that is, executive, legislative, and judicial – at all levels within the society. It is not just the president, the US Congress, and federal judges. It includes the state-level offices and all the way down to the local counties, cities, municipalities, and towns. It includes the staff from clerks to cabinet-level positions and can even include the custodial staff that cleans the building (if that service is not provided by another contracted business). It includes the men and women who enforce the laws (local police and deputies, even dog catchers) and all those involved in prosecuting, defending, and overseeing those proceedings, such as attorneys, judges, and court clerks. It includes the men and women who keep our nation safe (those in the military, FBI, and CIA). It includes those who oversee elections. It includes *most* government employees. *Most*, not all, because those teaching or working in public schools and universities are paid by the government, but are in the Education Mountain. Similarly, those in government-funded medical or social programs (like VA hospitals or child services) are in the Family Mountain.

"Everyone, especially Christians, is called to take part in government at some level."

This Mountain is extremely important because it writes – and enforces – the laws that affect *every* Mountain. Solomon got it right in Proverbs 29:2 when he said, "When the righteous are in authority, the people rejoice; But when a wicked man rules, the people groan." Michael Maiden provides a definition of "Your Duties in Government."

> Everyone, especially Christians, is called to take part in government at some level. We should all keep ourselves knowledgeable about current affairs, know what our government is doing, know about bills being proposed and

> passed, be familiar with the people who presently hold positions of power locally and nationally, and know about those running for office. And we should vote for the people who best represent our Christian principles and beliefs regardless of party affiliation.[75]

This is something that should be taught in every church and every ministry training program. If we are going to influence our culture, the Church *must* get its head out of the proverbial sand, get informed, stay informed, speak up, and take action. Many Christians are called to engage in this Mountain in even greater ways. How will we have righteous in authority if they do not step up to run for office? Thank God for those who have answered that call. That number is growing, but more are needed at all levels of government. It takes time and a lengthy process to rise to upper levels of influence in any realm. We need a constant flow of people called by God in the pipeline in each Mountain going through the training, learning, and experiences needed to rise to the top.

Chapter 6
Synergizing the Perspectives

Now that we understand each Mountain, this chapter will provide a brief recap of the journey of the two primary ambassadors in their efforts to see true transformation in cities, regions, and nations. It will then show how their two messages synergize and conclude with an action plan and a reminder of the overarching Kingdom principles that must always guide our actions.

Both Lance Wallnau and Johnny Enlow felt the frustration of knowing that transformation was God's intent and yet not seeing it. Their paths were different, yet they ended up in the same place. They came from different perspectives and walked different paths to get to the same truth. Since we have yet to see transformation on a large scale, there may yet be more revealed, especially with respect to strategy and methods. At a minimum, we have not yet implemented what we now understand on a large enough scale here in the United States to see the impact we seek. The steps outlined in the plan presented reflect the current revelation. We still have much to do just in bringing this teaching into mainstream Christianity and implementing what we know.

It should be noted that at the time Wallnau and Enlow were experiencing so much frustration (from the late 1990s into the 2000s), George Otis, Jr., was releasing a series of "Transformation" videos. Each video told the story of a city or rural region where people prayed, had an encounter with God, and then saw their city or area transformed. These reports may have contributed to the driving desire by both Wallnau and Enlow to see transformation occurring not occasionally, here or there, as was being reported by George Otis, but consistently. It seems safe to assume they would have been aware of Otis and his work, including the videos. The level of impact it had on either of them is unknown.

Recapping the Journeys

Lance Wallnau heard about the Seven Mountain revelation from Loren Cunningham (as revealed to Cunningham and Bill Bright) in 2000. He researched it, studied it, and began teaching it and consulting based on its principles. He changed the terminology from "mind-molders" or "world systems" to "mountains" and coined the term "Seven Mountain Mandate."

After more than a decade, ***Wallnau was frustrated with*** the lack of fruit, specifically, ***the lack of transformation for cities or nations***. After all, this revelation came as the answer to how to disciple nations. Why were they not changing?

Wallnau understood spiritual warfare and had practiced it to deal with demonic powers interfering with businesses with which he was consulting. He recognized that this needed to be done on a larger scale to bring breakthrough to larger territories – like a whole Mountain or a city. He believed his missing piece was the need for believers to band together in micro churches within each of the Mountains (or, potentially, across Mountains for similar roles). Together, they could gain the momentum and strength – by synergy and force multiplication – to bring down the demonic spirits ruling in each sphere. ***Transformation would begin with spiritual warfare to drive out the demonic control so that the territory could then be occupied.***

Johnny Enlow began ministering in Peru in 1995. He witnessed hundreds, and then thousands, of salvations, healings, and miracles. In 1999, the level of those continued to increase as he also began to see the impact of the fulfillment of prophetic words spoken to government leaders, which would bolster the economy of their city or region. God was showing His goodness in a new way. But ***Enlow was frustrated with the lack of*** impact on the societal structures that would bring real ***transformation for cities and nations***, thereby truly impacting the lives of the people on every level.

His missing piece turned out to be the Seven Mountain message itself. Unlike Wallnau, who heard this message from someone else, Enlow's revelation came to him directly, through a series of nightly encounters with God in 2006. It started with Holy Spirit showing him how the seven nations identified in Deuteronomy 7 (the "ites") that Israel had to conquer in their Promised Land to possess their inheritance were correlated to the seven societal structures. He also began to refer to these as "mountains." Holy Spirit revealed the principality that had ruled each of these nations and is ruling its associated Mountain today.[*] The starting point was that the "ites" (principalities and demonic strongholds) in each Mountain would have to be conquered (cast down) before transformation would be seen and sustained. ***Transformation would begin with spiritual warfare to drive out the demonic control so that the territory could then be occupied.***

Reaching the Same Place

Both men reached the same place. We must deal with the demonic powers that are controlling each sphere before we can truly occupy the territory. This is true whether that is an individual business, a department within a business, or an entire Mountain. While these illustrations focus on business, understand that this is applicable in any Mountain. For example, in the Mountain of Education, the sphere might be a state-wide curriculum, a school board, a specific school, or an individual classroom within that school. It is equally applicable,

---

[*] Holy Spirit showed Johnny Enlow much more about each Mountain than is addressed in this book. See *RISE: A Reformer's Handbook for the Seven Mountains* for additional details.

regardless of the Mountain; translate it to your Mountain or your sphere of influence within that Mountain.

While the need for spiritual warfare has been emphasized, it is the starting point, not the end of the matter.

Before we can possess the Mountain, we must drive the "ites" out of it. We must deal with the "rulers of darkness of this age." That is our starting point. Ephesians 6:12 tells us: "For we do not wrestle against flesh and blood, but against principalities, against powers, against the rulers of the darkness of this age, against spiritual hosts of wickedness in the heavenly places." We are not warring against flesh and blood, but against the spiritual wickedness *that is affecting the flesh and blood people* with whom we must interact. Fortunately, we know that "the weapons of our warfare are not carnal but mighty in God for pulling down strongholds," (2 Corinthians 10:4).

Implementing the Plan

While the need for spiritual warfare has been emphasized, it is the starting point, not the end of the matter. Even before you engage in warfare, you must identify your assigned place and get into it. The plan outlined below covers all the points that have been spread throughout the book. It is a summary of the steps for reclaiming territory, be that an entire Mountain or a segment of one.

1. **Get in position.** Each believer needs to identify the Mountain(s) to which they are called and the place(s) they are meant to occupy and get into position. Your place within a given Mountain will change over time and even the Mountain of your primary focus may change over time. This will be discussed more in Chapter 10.

2. **Identify your tribe.** Within that Mountain or your sphere of influence in it, each believer should identify their "tribe" of like-minded believers. Find other believers with a similar understanding (or open to it) and band together as a micro church so you can turn that synergy into force multiplication in your effectiveness. In addition to those with whom you work, network with others of similar calls, either in the same Mountain or in a similar role in a different Mountain, through training events and networking organizations.

3. **Identify the *spiritual* enemy.** Identify the enemy, the demonic forces controlling or trying to control that sphere of influence. The Enlows provide a list of the overarching principality for each Mountain in *RISE*[76]. If you are operating anywhere within a given Mountain, you are going to see the effects of that principality. However, there will be other demonic spirits all up and down the Mountains that partner with that principality. Focus on your sphere of influence. What are the demonic influences there? What are the dominant lies being believed? What is the false narrative that needs to be corrected?

4. **Wage a good warfare.** Wage a good warfare in the spirit, break down any demonic strongholds, and drive all evil spirits out. Begin to speak the truth in place of the lie. Speak the correct narrative, the message God wants to deliver. Use your weapons of spiritual warfare to wage an effective war against evil. Evict (cast out) the demons that are interfering at your level. (See 2 Corinthians 10:4-6 and Ephesians 6:10-18.) Be sure to release the counterpart spirit and expression of the Kingdom of God in their place.

5. **Stay in your lane.** Be sure to stay within your own level of spiritual authority. Individuals should never presume to take on a principality. Those are usually addressed by apostolic-prophetic teams after much intercession and warfare and *only*

at the direction of Holy Spirit. If everyone does their part, dealing with the demonic spirits all up and down the mountain will weaken the strongholds at the top. That will make the final casting down of that principality much easier. *Do the part God calls you to do.* Do not allow fear or any other excuse to cause you to fail to do your part. Each part is needed. Know that God will always back you up when you move in obedience to do what He has called you to do. Conversely, do not try to do someone else's part. You are only anointed to do your part. Stepping out of your lane and into someone else's can have undesirable repercussions.

6. **Shine your light.** Allow the light of the Kingdom of God to be shed abroad wherever you are and wherever you go. Operate out of Kingdom principles and teach them to others. That is what Jesus instructed us to do in Matthew 28:19-20. We often talk about "pushing back darkness." Just turn on the light and darkness must retreat; it has no choice. One candle may not offer much light. As you connect with your micro church and then teach others how to operate using these principles, your combined light begins to bring much more illumination. We will again see the effect of synergy where the combined light is much more than the sum of the individual candles.

7. **Occupy your territory.** Too often, we gain ground only to back off and turn it back over to the enemy, requiring another battle to regain it all over again. Revelation 2:25 tells us to "hold fast what you have till I come." We need to be like Shammah in 2 Samuel 23:11-12 who stood his ground in the middle of the field and defended it against the Philistines. Remain vigilant and do not allow the enemy to recapture your territory.

Adhering to Our Principles

In looking at these implementation steps, we should always keep the following principles in mind. These principles are what make us different from other religions and ideologies, what sets us apart. To bring Kingdom influence, we must operate out of Kingdom principles.

- **We operate with God's wisdom and prophetic insight to bring solutions to problems others cannot solve.** God is creative and He wants to impart His creative ideas to His children. This will include new inventions, discoveries, and more in every sphere, but we must seek and rely on His wisdom and creativity.
- **The further up the mountain we go, the more people we serve, including those in other mountains.** We serve; we never lord over others. We realize that ruling over others was never God's plan and Jesus showed us by example that the greatest among us is the servant of all. We must always seek to model servanthood, even when strong leadership is needed. Meekness is not weakness; it is controlled strength. Being a servant of the people does not mean being weak or indecisive; Jesus was neither. Jesus was very confrontational when dealing with evil. The motive for confrontation or standing one's ground should be for righteousness' sake and the good of the people. It should never be because of ego, self-righteousness, or self-promotion.
- **We shift the culture through influence, never force.** The resolution to societal problems through God-ordained solutions and how we treat others, ruling with a servant's heart, will both become apparent. It is the impact of the solutions we bring and the way we treat others that we shift opinions, which will shift culture.

Functioning "As One"

In closing this section, I want to reiterate the importance of coming together and working together. Anyone who has listened to Lance Wallnau for long knows that he loves to refer to a particular scene in *The Gladiator*, a movie released in 2000. In it, Maximus realizes that he and the other gladiators with him in the arena are about to be overrun by Roman soldiers in chariots. The scene is to be a re-enactment of a battle in which the Romans defeated "the barbarians" in the battle of Carthage. The expectation is that the gladiators will all be slaughtered as the Carthaginians had been. Maximus, a former Roman general, quickly devices a plan of not just survival, but victory. It required the cooperation of the other gladiators. Their key to survival was working together, "as one," which was also the verbal cue to do so. Through a series of military maneuvers in which they locked their shields and raised them in unison at the correct angle at just the right moment, they overturned speeding chariots. Their teamwork turned the battle, which turned the crowd's favor toward them.

"As One!" became Wallnau's ending battle cry for many of his sessions emphasizing the need for unity. I believe that should still be our battle cry. We need to lock our shields of faith and raise them together. We must not allow our minor differences to override the key objective of bringing the will of the Father, as it is done in heaven, to earth, so that the kingdoms of this world (today's world systems) shall become the kingdoms of our Lord and of His Christ. (See Revelation 11:15.) May His body, which should be fitly joined together, begin to truly function "As One!"

Section 2

Five-Fold Ministry in the Mountains

Chapter 7

Five-Fold Ministry Gifts in the Religion Mountain

One of the aspects that Johnny and Elizabeth Enlow included for each Mountain in *RISE* was which of the five-fold ministry gifts identified in Ephesians 4:11 (apostles, prophets, evangelists, pastors, and teachers) was most prevalent in each Mountain. You can find that information in their book.[77] I want to look at this from a different perspective.

As I have studied and pondered this topic over the years, I began to ask how each of the five-fold ministry gifts *intersects with* or *is manifested in* each of the Mountains. My underlying belief is that the characteristics of each are in each Mountain, just not in the way we normally think of them (if, in fact, we think of them at all). In addressing this, we must start with the underlying assumption that the reader believes in or at least acknowledges the roles of the five-fold ministry gifts in operation today. If not, please read on; it may help you see these roles in a new light.

As stated previously, I believe the Religion Mountain should touch all the other Mountains. More specifically, the Church should touch every Mountain. I also believe the five-fold ministry gifts (the people who are called and function as apostles, prophets, evangelists, pastors, and teachers) within the Church should touch each of the other Mountains. For that reason, I am beginning this discussion with the operation of these gifts specific to the Christian Church in the Religion Mountain.

First, we need a common understanding of how each of the five ministry gifts operates in its own Mountain. This topic can fill a book – in fact, there are many books already written about it and they do not necessarily agree. For purposes of this book, I am going to try to keep this simple, knowing that even then there will be some disagreement. However, we need a mutual understanding of each role within the Church so that we can then look at how it functions in the other Mountains. For a more in-depth explanation of the five-fold ministry and how it should operate under a New Testament model, I recommend *Kingdom Function of the Five-Fold Ministry and Church Government* by Dr. Greg Hood. It is available through Greg Hood Ministries (at https://www.greghood.org/). The summary here aligns with his much more detailed explanations.

The first shift you will have to make, if you have not already done so, is to realize that the way we use the term "pastor" as the senior leader in the local church or any "minister" on the "pastoral staff" is scripturally incorrect. In fact, the only reference to the word "pastor" in the New Testament is in Ephesians 4:11 when Paul, referring to Christ, says, "And He Himself gave some to be apostles, some prophets, some evangelists, and some pastors and teachers." "Pastor" is translated from the Greek word "poimen"[78] and means "a herdsman, especially a shepherd."[79]

The role of the pastor is that of shepherd; that is how "poimen" is translated in every other instance in the New Testament. Nowhere in the New Testament is a pastor (or shepherd) appointed to oversee a church. When Paul established a local body, it would be elders (plural) who were appointed to oversee it in his absence. (See Acts 14:23 and Titus 1:5.) In brief, the elders are one of the five-fold ministry gifts identified in 1 Corinthians 12:28, which does not include either evangelists or pastors. This will be explained a little more later. The concept of and requirements for elders are discussed at length by Dr. Hood in his book referenced above.

Apostles

With that background, let us look at a couple of key scriptures. The first is Ephesians 2:19-20, which says, "... the household of God, having been *built on the foundation of the apostles and prophets*, Jesus Christ Himself being the chief cornerstone." (Emphasis added.) This passage states that "the household of God," a local group that meets together to worship God, needs to have both the apostolic and prophetic ministry imparting into it to have a solid foundation.

The apostle sees the big picture. He has the vision for where God intends the ministry he oversees to head. He will need assistance from the other five-fold ministry gifts as well as the saints to get there, but he is the one with the vision; he sees the destination. And before the ministry reaches one goal, he sees three more! He is a visionary and a dreamer who will always be looking toward the next thing(s).

The apostle sees the big picture.

Apostles are often pioneers, going where no one else has gone before. That may be geographical (as was often the case with the apostles in the New Testament and is still true of some missionary apostles today). Or it may be in doing new things in new ways to spread the gospel. They are often the ones trying out the latest technology. "Change" is their middle name. As they try new things, if something does not work well, they have no problem abandoning that idea to try the next one. If you like the status quo and keeping things the same, they will frustrate you.

Apostles sometimes function in more than one office at a time, especially when they are pioneering. For example, if a missionary apostle goes into an unreached territory geographically, he may function in all five roles until there are others raised up to come alongside with the other giftings. The same can be true when planting a new church or starting a new ministry. To function that way over the long term will take its toll; God did not intend one person to do everything. That is why Jesus gave us all five ministry gifts and the saints to do "the work of the ministry" (Ephesians 4:12). Ephesians 2:19-20 tells us that both the apostle and the prophet are needed to build a proper foundation for the work; every work that wants a solid foundation must have both.

Prophets

Of course, the prophet can foresee and foretell things that will happen. This foundational role is much more than that. The prophet is often the one who can identify the strategy needed to fulfill the vision of the apostle. As the visionary, the apostle sees where he wants to go; as the strategist, the prophet can help him plot a course to get there. Prophets are wired to see both potential dangers and potential opportunities.

> *The prophet is often the one that can identify the strategy needed to fulfill the vision of the apostle.*

Further, the God-inspired words of a prophet can break spiritual bondages and strongholds. As apostles are pioneering, they need the breakthrough anointing of the prophet to shift atmospheres and break through spiritual barriers. Sometimes a prophet needs "to root out and pull down, to destroy and to throw down" (Jeremiah 1:10) before a proper foundation can be built.

Another thing that prophets often do is either impart or identify and confirm a specific anointing on individuals. This helps in getting the right people identified and set in the right place within a ministry or even in the larger corporate body of Christ.

As the work progresses, the prophet is usually the one with the keenest sense of discerning of spirits. He can smell a rat (or spot a wolf) long before there is any evidence that there is one in your midst – or trying to intrude. Providing this insight to the apostle can be invaluable, sparing a lot of potential damage or at least stopping it as soon as it starts. It is usually the apostle who would then decide when and how to address it. The apostle usually carries a greater leadership anointing and authority. Nonetheless, these two must work together with mutual respect to be effective. When they work *well* together, you might sometimes wonder which is in which role. The apostle can move prophetically, and the prophet can sometimes provide vision (by foreseeing) to the apostle and leadership to others on the team.

Teachers

In 1 Corinthians 12:28, Paul gives the "next steps" after the apostle and prophet. Notice that he is clear on the order of the first three. "God has appointed these in the church: *first* apostles, *second* prophets, *third* teachers, after that, miracles, then gifts of healings, helps, administrations, varieties of tongues." (Emphasis added.) The terms used here for "first," "second," and "third," are ordinal numbers. They are the Greek words "protos," "deuteros," and "tritos."[80] "Protos" means "first in time or place" or "first in rank;"[81] "deuteros" means "the second, the other of two;"[82] and "tritos" means "the third."[83] Order is intended. Here it is indisputable that, for any church to function properly, the first role required is an apostle, the second is a prophet, and the third is a teacher.

The apostle does not necessarily have to remain part of the local work that is established. Paul did not. But, like Paul, there should be an apostle who is involved with, offering counsel to, and overseeing the work. There would need to be an appropriate eldership in place that relates to and communicates regularly with the overseeing apostle. "After that," there are several other gifts needed for the local church to function well. They are all needed; the order in which they are identified or added is not crucial.

Here it is indisputable that, for any church to function properly, the first role required is an apostle, the second role is a prophet, and the third is a teacher.

The role of teacher is more easily understood. Teachers bring understanding and cover content in orderly, methodical ways. We need those who understand and are solidly grounded in the Word and who are gifted to teach it in a way that is understood and can be applied by everyone in the local body, regardless of their current experience and knowledge level.

A true teacher loves to research and study a topic, so they know when they are teaching that they have all their facts straight. They like to make sure "i's are dotted and t's are crossed." In the Church world, they will dig into the Hebrew or Greek to capture the nuance the translator missed. Then they know how to convey what they have learned at a level appropriate to their audience.

Their reward is when they see the "light bulb" come on in their students. Their real thrill comes when they see the student apply what they have learned. That is when they know that the student truly "got it." The teacher may be part of the local body, or they may be itinerant, coming in to teach a particular topic or series. Often, there is a mixture of the two.

The remainder of that verse ("after that miracles, then gifts of healings, helps, administrations, varieties of tongues") can cause challenges. Most local churches understand and have the gifts of helps (usually volunteers) and administration (someone who tends to the business side of things). Unfortunately, the other three gifts, which were obviously common in the early church, are often missing. Even the Pentecostal and charismatic churches today rarely have "varieties of tongues" demonstrated in a service. Hopefully, this is occurring during prayer services and at other times. Likewise, many churches never see any real healings, let alone miracles, in their midst. These, of course, do not have to happen during a service; they can occur anytime, anywhere. Unfortunately, they are still too uncommon rather than being the norm.

Evangelists

What of the evangelists and pastors? Evangelists are fishermen. They love to catch fish and pull them into the Kingdom, using the good news of the gospel as their bait. It does not matter if that is one-on-one at the local mall, in a coffee shop, or while filling their car up with gas or if it is in a mass crusade where hundreds or thousands accept Christ.

Evangelists are fishermen.

They need to be associated with a local church, so the fish they catch have somewhere to go and be turned into sheep. Discipling is neither their forte nor their passion. Their thrill is in the catch – a soul brought into the Kingdom. Every local church needs evangelists. Growth should primarily be made up of new believers, not simply membership transfers. The evangelist should also be teaching the believers in the local body how to evangelize. While we may not be called and gifted as a five-fold ministry gift evangelist, we should all know how to lead someone to the Lord and be doing so.

We need to understand that not everyone in the Church who loves to *evangelize* – witness and win people to the Lord – is a five-fold *evangelist*. Ephesians 4:11-12 is clear that the five ministry gifts identified are "for the equipping of the saints for the work of the ministry." The five-fold gifts should be equipping (teaching and training) the saints (the Christians) how to minister effectively. If someone is evangelizing but not training others how to do so (or in other aspects of their Christian walk), they are a soul-winner ministering to others the gift of salvation as the evangelist (or others) have taught them to do. We should *all* be soul-winners, but we are not all evangelists.

Pastors

Discipleship is the key role of the pastors. The pastors (shepherds) are the ones who have the extra measure of love and compassion (and patience!) to deal with all the problems that sheep tend to have. They are the ones who can help them grow at the speed they can manage. That may mean teaching them the same principles over and over until they "get it" or picking them back up repeatedly until they are completely set free and their walk stabilized. They are sensitive to the speed at which a given lamb can travel and know how to urge them forward without pushing them too hard. They make sure the sheep are fed a well-balanced diet of the whole counsel of the Word of God and not allowed to solely feed on a favorite topic.

Discipleship is the key role of the pastors.

If a sheep disappears (begins not showing up for services or group meetings), it is the true shepherd who notices their absence and starts reaching out to find them and determine what is wrong. It is the shepherd who hurries to the hospital or goes to the home of someone who has lost a loved one. The shepherd makes sure the elderly person not only has a ride to services but also someone helping them get their groceries and clean their house. They are the ones constantly calling, texting, or messaging various people just to check on them. They *genuinely care* about people. They spend time with them and get to know them and their family.

They get satisfaction from knowing all their sheep are receiving the care they need. Their thrill is seeing a believer growing and maturing in their walk with the Lord and beginning to minister effectively to others around them.

Touching the Other Mountains

How do these five-fold ministry giftings manifest in each of the other Mountains? There are touchpoints from the Church in the Religion Mountain to the other Mountains for each of the five-fold ministry roles. However, we also see those who *look like* they fill these roles in each of the other Mountains when in fact they are not truly apostles, prophets, evangelists, pastors, or teachers as defined in Ephesians 4. Rather, they have the same *characteristics*, meaning the same motivational gifts and personality traits.

As we look at the other Mountains, we will investigate how the *characteristics* of each of these five roles are reflected in each of the other Mountains. Then we will take another look at all five ministry gifts within the Church and how each may *intersect* with the other Mountains.

Chapter 8

Five-Fold Characteristics in the Other Mountains

Characteristics of Apostles

On any Mountain, there will always be the visionaries, pressing the envelope to do new things. These are the pioneers. The *character traits* and often personalities of these people will be very much like those of the apostle. The difference is in what they are called (or destined) to do. While the focus of the apostle is equipping the saints and expanding the Kingdom of God, the focus of the visionary in the other Mountains will be expanding their sphere.

For Media, that may be methods, mediums, and venues of communicating. For Family, which includes medical services, that might be breaking barriers in medical research with new innovative cures, such as light and sound that are only recently being openly discussed. For Arts & Entertainment, it could be new mediums of expression. For Business, the ideas are endless, especially since there are businesses in *every* Mountain. For Economy, as this is being written, we are seeing innovative measures being implemented nationally and internationally designed to get our nation back on a sound fiscal footing. For Education, it might be new teaching methods that improve the students' ability to learn. For Government, I pray that the visions implemented here in America take us back to a government of the people, by the people, and for the people, based on our original Judeo-Christian roots and our Constitution that was written from that perspective. We need innovative ideas coupled with divine intervention to get back there and, especially, to end the divisiveness and reunite us as a people who can once again express differing opinions without hatred.

> *While the focus of the apostle is equipping the saints and expanding the Kingdom of God, the focus of the visionary in the other Mountains will be expanding their sphere.*

If the visionary is a true disciple of Christ, he should always be looking for ways of expanding the Kingdom of God. Their primary way of expanding it is by operating out of its principles, operating in righteousness. What makes them tick is what they do in their particular area of expertise. The visionary may be the owner or CEO of a company who has highly skilled engineers and technicians pushing the limits to bring his vision into reality. Or he may be the technical genius looking for a financier to back the development of his new idea. Either way, visionaries are the ones who can see the possibilities of what the future could look like. This is true of a visionary, regardless of the Mountain.

In a large organization, there will be multiple visionaries. As an example we can all understand, every secretary who serves on the cabinet of the president of the United States is a visionary in their area of expertise. To be effective, their vision must align with the president's overall vision. If it does not, they must adjust it to do so or there will be conflicts. If a person, regardless of the Mountain, does not believe they can fully align with the vision of the leader, the right thing to do is step down and step away before there is conflict. In a corporation in any Mountain, these may be the various vice presidents or chief executive officers, or they may be directors or other leaders under them. Some of the visionaries at the lower levels today will be the ones leading tomorrow. Each has been selected because of their expertise and because they are visionaries in their field. But their vision must align with the overall vision of the leader of the organization for them to be successful, personally, and for the overall company to be successful.

This is true even in the Religion Mountain. In a large organization (whether a denomination, a network of churches, or a para-church ministry of some sort), there will be apostles focused on one aspect of the ministry working under a lead or overseeing apostle. It is the overseeing apostle who carries the overall vision. If those laboring with him do not fully share his vision for their area of responsibility, there will eventually be a parting of ways. Regardless of the Mountain, it is much better to do that as soon as the differences are recognized, and peaceably, rather than staying and believing you will change the leader's vision. That is like marrying someone believing you will change them after the wedding.

Another element that should be understood is that the talents and personality traits that are imparted to us as one or more of the gifts listed in Romans 12:6-8 also come into play. Quoting:

> [6] *Having then gifts differing according to the grace that is given to us, let us use them: if prophecy, let us prophesy in proportion to our faith;* [7] *or ministry, let us use it in our ministering; he who teaches, in teaching;* [8] *he who exhorts, in exhortation; he who gives, with liberality; he who leads, with diligence; he who shows mercy, with cheerfulness.*

The gifts listed here are those innate talents and abilities placed in us by God at the time of our conception and help determine our likes, dislikes, and even personality. These are often called the "motivational gifts" because they are what motivate us to do much of what we do. An apostle will have the ability to lead, as will a successful CEO. In looking at the characteristics of the five-fold gifts, realize that some of those same or similar characteristics are coming from the motivational gifts. After all, those who have five-fold ministry gifts are also people, and we all have some mix of the motivational gifts.

Characteristics of Prophets

The counterpart to the prophet in the other Mountains is the strategist, whether they have that title or anyone ever uses that term. Just as the prophet helps the apostle fulfill his vision, this role in the other mountains helps the visionary fulfill his. This person is often "the right-hand man" (or woman) of the visionary, the one who understands his vision and can see how to make the vision a reality. The title for that role may vary from Mountain to Mountain and even from company to company within a given Mountain. Regardless of the title, every visionary needs a good strategist, just as every apostle needs a close relationship with a prophet.

Every "idea man" needs a good "reality guy" that he trusts with whom to collaborate.

The prophets see both potential opportunities and potential dangers in the spirit realm for a ministry. This role identifies the potential opportunities and problems ahead for the business or entity within which it is operating. They see the "what if's" and can work through them. Always seeing the potential problems can come across as being negative. Done properly, they provide a potential solution, either to avoid the issue or, if it is unavoidable, a way to navigate through it and mitigate the risk. Having this type of person collaborating with a visionary can mean the difference between success and failure. Every "idea man" needs a good "reality guy" that he trusts with whom to collaborate. As with the apostle and prophet, the visionary and the strategist need to have strong mutual respect; they must trust each other's gifting as well as each other's knowledge and expertise.

Prophets tend to see in black and white and always function "by the book." Other roles where you might find these personality characteristics are in the quality area or other areas requiring audits and in the area of security, including both physical safety and cybersecurity. Their propensity for being able to smell a rat before seeing any evidence of one is beneficial in these areas. Their "by the book" inner compass will not allow something to pass a quality check or audit unless it fully meets the specification. Their staunch view of things as black or white without any "shades of gray" will not allow cutting corners or approving anything that is questionable in any way. Though often viewed as inflexible, there are areas where consistency, reliability, and always doing things "by the book" are necessary traits, especially in areas that are highly audited or involve safety. These characteristics are also often common for those with the gift of prophecy in Romans 12:6. This reference is not to a prophet as found in Ephesians 4:11. Rather, it references the gift of prophecy, which is found in 1 Corinthians 12:10.

Characteristics of Teachers

In general, there is always training needed regardless of the field. For some, there is more than others. Obviously, a medical doctor requires more training than someone running a t-shirt shop or delivering grocery orders. Any formal training would occur in the Education Mountain, whether it is for a medical doctor or for an auto mechanic. Of course, the Education Mountain is filled with teachers. But there is training within each Mountain, requiring instructors, whether they are truly gifted as teachers or not.

For example, a business of any size, regardless of the Mountain in which it resides, will have some "in -service" training for employees. This will start with some training during the onboarding process, even if that is simply how to record daily time, report absences, and request time off. That is usually done by Human Resources (HR) in any company large enough to have an HR department. In a smaller business, it may be the immediate manager or supervisor. Likewise, most companies of any size have additional employee training on any number of topics, including technical skills, leadership skills, laws or regulations related to the business, and safety training. This is sometimes provided by HR or whoever within the company is the subject matter expert for technical skills; sometimes, a third-party training company is brought in.

A true teacher is always "looking to see" if the pupil is understanding.

If an outside company provides the training, it might reside in the Education Mountain, or, if it is specific to the industry, it might reside in the same Mountain as the companies it services. For example, a company that prepares employees to pass a certification exam within a specific industry might reside fully within that same Mountain, if that is the only type of training the company provides. Conversely, a company that prepares someone who has just finished the formal education process for a professional exam for licensure would be tied to the educational process in the Education Mountain.

There may be other needs for specialized training within a business. A manufacturing plant will need to train a new employee or even an internal transfer for their specific position. Even if they have gone to a technical school for general training, they will need to know the specifics of how to create and check the part for which they are responsible. A nurse may have a B.S.N. with years of experience. In taking a new position, there will be training in how that organization does things, especially administrative procedures. Even an experienced cashier taking a job at a different company will need to know the specifics of where to find information, how to use the new company's computerized register versus what they may have used before, and the specific check-in and check-out procedure for the register.

Bottom line, *instructors* are needed everywhere. However, not all of those who provide instruction in such cases will have the gift of teaching. They may go through a checklist or set of instructions that has been developed for them without having the driving desire to impart knowledge and make sure the student is understanding it. It is a duty they have been given to perform. A true teacher is always "looking to see" if the pupil is understanding. If not, they will find an alternate way of saying what they are trying to get across or a different analogy that will make more sense to that individual.

In some ways, a teacher in any of the other Mountains, and particularly in the Mountain of Education, can look much (if not exactly) like a teacher in the Mountain of Religion or vice versa. What is different is the content they teach. Also, the teacher in any of the Mountains, Religion included, might be showing characteristic traits from the gift of teaching found in Romans 12:7 rather than being a teacher as identified in Ephesians 4.

Hopefully, the teacher in the Religion Mountain is called and anointed by God with that ministry gift. The same *should* be true for those called as a teacher into any of the Mountains – and for any position in any Mountain. That is the key to this message, *finding what God has destined and gifted us to do and doing it* – in whichever Mountain or Mountains that may take us.

Characteristics of Evangelists

Evangelists like to share the good news. In the Church, that is the good news of the gospel with the hope of it ending in a salvation. In most other Mountains, it is the good news about the product or service that they offer with the hope of it ending in a sale. Hence, the role corresponding to the evangelist is usually found in the sales and marketing department.

The salesmen are the ones who find all the ways to tell you how wonderful their product is. It does not matter whether they are promoting a movie, a car, a new dental office, the latest technology gadget, or a new supplement that will cure all your woes. A true salesman will tell anyone and everyone about the product or service they are promoting. Just go to dinner or out for coffee with one and you will quickly find out.

This can be a place where you see overlap from the visionary role into the marketing role, just as an apostle also evangelizes. (Think of Paul or any of the other apostles in Acts.) The visionary is excited about his products. Visionaries are often most excited about the product that is *coming*. That can cause a dilemma when the new product is still in development, and they cannot openly talk about it yet!

All who work in the Media Mountain are engaged in evangelism (spreading the news) to a degree.

The Media Mountain is a bit of an exception here. Media *should* be fulfilling a similar role to the evangelist in that it *should* be sharing good news about events, not just gloom and despair meant to drive fear and anxiety. As the Enlows put it so well, "Media that blesses presents truth through a hopeful perspective that gives the listener the ability to envision a happy ending, even when it's news that is difficult to hear."[84] It is not a matter of ignoring bad news; it is finding the good that can come from it and talking about that as well. For too long, this Mountain has specialized in drama, crises, and catastrophes. "Bad news" is their specialty; the more shocking, the better. It is time to turn that around to truth conveyed with hope.

As previously discussed, there are outlets where this is now happening, and more are springing up constantly. In fact, while writing this section, I saw an ad on Facebook for *The Pour Over* (at https://thepourover.org/). Their ad, which is no longer accessible, led with, "News doesn't have to mean impending doom." It continued, "Join 1M+ Christians who start their week *with hope-filled headlines* from The Pour Over." (Emphasis added.) On their website, their byline reads, "The News You Need. The Peace You Crave," with a subline saying, "Politically Neutral, Christ-First News." This obviously targets a Christian audience. Others, like *The Epoch Times*, do not necessarily. It takes people with a hopeful outlook (i.e., Christians who understand Kingdom) getting involved in this Mountain in ways that reach out to all, not just the Christian audience. We need evangelists who bring good news.

Another Mountain where this expresses itself a little differently is the Mountain of Government. Here, the evangelistic role overlaps with the Media Mountain in that the primary evangelist for the top of the Government Mountain (in the United States, the president) is the White House press secretary. That is the role that helps broadcast and sell what the president wants done. At lower levels in government, it is often the leader going directly to the press. For example, the speaker of the House or one of the majority or minority leaders in Congress will hold a press briefing after a major decision or when they are trying to garner support for one. They are evangelizing their agenda or selling their solution. Similarly, at the state and local levels, governors and other state leaders use press conferences or interviews with the press to evangelize their message or sell their platform.

All who work in the Media Mountain are engaged in evangelism (spreading the news) to a degree. May God raise up more of His people to be engaged there so that the news relayed to the people is truthful, accurate, and always laced with hope.

Characteristics of Pastors

Last, but not least, is the role of pastor. In the Church, they are the ones who disciple. Pastors are the ones who really get to know those under their care and help them become better at what they do or grow into new roles. They are patient with those who are learning and maturing in their walk with the Lord and work with them in whatever way needed to facilitate that. Pastors are "people people." In the other Mountains, someone who has the same characteristics looks much the same. These may be evidence of the motivation gifts from Romans 12, such as ministry (or serving), exhorting (or encouraging), showing mercy, and giving rather than a five-fold ministry gift.

Pastors are the ones who really get to know those under their care and help them become better at what they do or grow into new roles.

In Business, these are typically supervisors, managers, or in Human Resources. In the Education Mountain, they are often the guidance counselors. In the Family Mountain, they may be social workers or counselors. In Arts & Entertainment, they may be talent agents or coaches. Wherever they are, they want to get to know their people. They want to encourage people and help them succeed individually as well as succeeding as a team or family. They are willing to facilitate an individual getting needed training and proper exposure. They are concerned when there are family problems or issues, even when they are not in the Family Mountain and not just because of it being distracting at work. If they truly have the pastor characteristics and motivational gifts, they are genuinely concerned about the person and their family.

These characteristics or gifts may be found in anyone within the workforce. It could be the office assistant who knows how to connect people with the resources (others within the organization or training) they need to help them succeed and grow. Or it could be an upper-level manager who loves seeing potential in others and helping them get what they need to develop it and succeed. In the Education Mountain, this can be a teacher or a coach who takes extra interest in the students. It could be a guidance counselor or someone in administration, such as a vice principal or principal. The main consideration within the work world is that this person must be able to take the time needed to get to know and counsel individuals and still fulfill their own job responsibilities.

Chapter 9

Five-Fold Ministry Gifts in the Mountains

In the last chapter, we discussed how the *characteristics* of each of the five-fold ministry gifts from the Mountain of Religion manifest on the other Mountains. Now we will take a quick look at how each of these gives ministry gifts *intersects* and interacts with the other Mountains.

Apostles in the Mountains

Apostles can pastor (disciple and care for) the heads of organizations in any of the Mountains in the same way they pastor the other five-fold ministry gifts who serve within their own organization. They can offer wisdom and godly counsel on both personal and professional issues. This may include how to manage difficult or uncomfortable situations, particularly when ethics are involved. Apostles provide sound counsel from outside the leader's normal peer group, which can bring a fresh perspective. At times, they may function as an impartial sounding board when there are issues within their leadership team. The apostle's counsel is based on Kingdom principles, not technical expertise. Technical expertise is the role of the leadership team and those who work for them.

Apostles can pastor the heads of organizations in any of the Mountains.

Because apostles are visionaries, they may sometimes assist the visionaries in the other Mountains by helping them formulate or clarify their vision while keeping it centered and grounded on godly principles. They may even challenge the visionary to enlarge his vision. The key is that the apostle continually points the visionary to Kingdom principles in all decision-making, even when he cannot say that is what he is doing.

Prophets in the Mountains

The prophet comes from a different perspective. One role is beautifully illustrated by the stories shared of Johnny Enlow's journey into understanding this message. He met with leaders of cities and spoke hope into their circumstances by sharing what God was going to reveal for their city or region. Eventually, Enlow was meeting with leaders of nations. He, Lance Wallnau, and other recognized prophets who understand this concept meet with both leaders of businesses and governmental leaders, including leaders of nations, in the US and around the globe. In most cases, you and I will never know what they tell them or even with whom they met or when, which is as it should be. Johnny Enlow was able to share what he has seen happen in Peru, with permission and documented proof, as a way of teaching others what can be done – what God *wants* to do.

Old Testament prophets spoke more to kings or directly to the people than they did to religious leaders.

There are also accounts of prophetic words of warning given to leaders. Again, these cannot and should not normally be shared publicly, unless the leader chooses to do so after the fact. One I will always remember was a word given to a business leader about someone embezzling from him. His business was doing well, and he trusted the leaders under him. He had no reason to suspect anything of the sort. Trusting the word of the prophet, he began to investigate and found his accountant had been embezzling for years, amassing quite a sum in an offshore account. Because this leader believed in bringing a prophet into his business and took seriously what was said, he experienced 2 Chronicles 20:20 firsthand: "… believe His prophets, and you shall prosper."

Prophets taking this role of warning, primarily within businesses in the various mountains or with government leaders, is quite Biblical. Old Testament prophets spoke more to kings or directly to the people than they did to religious leaders. One New Testament example of speaking to both the government and a businessman is found in Acts 27:9-11. In this passage, Paul warned the centurion and, through him, both the owner and the captain of the ship not to set sail from Fair Haven until spring. He warned that if they did, "this voyage will end with disaster and much loss, not only of the cargo and ship, but also our lives." We know that the cargo and the ship were lost; for Paul's sake, God spared all the people.

As mentioned in Chapter 3, Lance Wallnau (a prophet/teacher) currently directs the Lance Learning Group, a strategic teaching and consulting company. In addition to that, he works with Ed Rush, another business consultant, to provide guidance for those who join their Mach10Masterminds group. (See edrush.com/coaching.) In a recent interview with Ed Rush on *The Lance Wallnau Show* regarding this group, Wallnau asked Rush to give a quick rundown of their high-level strategy. Here are the four key components as outlined by Rush (paraphrased)[85]:

> **#1: God's Wisdom** – Start with Divine wisdom. Always ask God your question or seek His counsel *first*, including for strategy.
>
> **#2: Man's Wisdom** – Ask for human wisdom. Ask people who "have been there, done that" and are *still* doing it.

#3: Prophetic – Put prophets or prophetic people around the businesspeople to speak the current word of the Lord to them.

#4: Prayer – Have a prayer team.

If you look at the qualifications for joining this group, you will see that these are serious, high-level businesspeople. Yet, notice the importance and value placed on having the prophetic operating with them. The apostle needs a close relationship with a prophet to accurately lay the foundation of a local church or ministry and grow it. Likewise, business leaders, regardless of the Mountain, need that relationship as well to see the full potential of their business and of themselves as businesspeople. We saw the value of that in the Government Mountain through Johnny Enlow's testimonies of what happened in Peru. (Point #4 speaks of the need for a micro church.)

Teachers in the Mountains

The function of the teacher is primarily in training the saints in the Church "for the work of ministry," (Ephesians 4:12). While all five-fold ministry gifts are to do this, the teacher is unique in that it is their primary role. The teacher who understands the Seven Mountain Mandate teaches believers how to go into the Mountain where they are called and impact it. This should be taught in every local church. (Refer back to Michael Maiden's "The Purpose of the Church" under the Religion Mountain in Chapter 5.)

There are teachers in the Church who are equipped to go into the other Mountains as consultants and train the leaders in the other Mountains in what we know as Kingdom principles. These teachers will not call what they are teaching "Kingdom principles" or even "Biblical principles." Nor will they reference them as coming from the Bible – unless, of course, the leadership of the organization embraces doing so. God's principles work, regardless of who exercises them or what they are called, just as gravity works regardless of whether one believes in it. These five-fold ministry gift teachers will teach leaders within the other Mountains to conduct their businesses using godly principles while not identifying the principles as such. Lance Wallnau was one of the early pioneers in this area, if not the first, and continues to teach and consult today.

There are teachers who are equipped to go into the other Mountains as a consultant and train the leaders in the other Mountains in Kingdom principles.

The other area of training needed for believers within the other Mountains is how to become people of influence within your Mountain. This is training targeted at those with leadership potential; the ones who have the potential of making it to top - level positions of influence in their Mountain. There are numerous groups now targeting this, such as Mach10Masterminds and The Pinnacle Forum (mentioned in Chapter 2). Another is the Christian Center for Public Life (CCPL) for Latin America, founded by Johnny and Elizabeth Enlow. It is included because of the previous discussion of their work in Latin America and because they are currently working to develop a similar program for the United States. Their end-of-year 2024 report on CCPL stated: "Over the past five years, we've graduated 279 sharp, Christian leaders from 22 Latin American countries, who are now positioned and prepared to serve and bring needed change in their nations."[86]

There are others who are already doing similar things in the US and elsewhere, as well as similar work in other Mountains. As a reminder, the Enlows have created the RISE Global Community application. It serves influencers in every area of society by providing a platform for communicating with others within their respective Mountain(s). (See https://www.rise7.org/the-global-community for information.)

What I am seeing, at least initially, is a blending of teachers (or in the case of both Lance Wallnau and Johnny Enlow, prophet/teachers) from the Religion Mountain, collaborating with leaders and teachers from the other Mountains to accomplish these types of schools. I do not know if that will eventually shift with those from the Religion Mountain stepping back as others step up to do this training. I do not believe that it will, at least not in the foreseeable future. I believe the insight from the Church – from both prophets and apostles – brought forth by teachers will always be needed in these efforts.

Evangelists in the Mountains

The evangelist's effect in these Mountains has been in a more indirect way. The evangelist should be teaching other believers how to fish – without scaring the fish away! A true evangelist will fish anywhere at any time. No matter how he interacts with any of the Mountains, he is always looking for someone who might be hungry for the gospel. However, an evangelist from the Religion Mountain will not have the day-to-day access to the people in these Mountains that those who interact there daily will have. His biggest impact has been in training those who are there, teaching them how to bait the hook and then know when and how to reel in the catch. This role will continue. Many Christians do not know how to lead someone to the Lord. This is a training deficiency in the Church that affects our effectiveness everywhere.

Evangelists who can share the gospel clearly, in a low-key, business-savvy sort of way, will be needed.

I said "has been" because this could, and I believe will, change. In the episode of *The Lance Wallnau Show* mentioned earlier, Wallnau spoke of envisioning groups of international business leaders starting to come together in meetings much like the Full Gospel Business Men's Fellowship International

(FGBMFI) meetings of the 1970s and 1980s.[87] In the FGBMFI meetings, Christian businessmen would invite their non- or nominal-Christian friends or associates to a nice dinner followed by a presentation of the gospel with an invitation to know Christ. Everything was done in a business-like atmosphere and manner. When these meetings Wallnau envisions begin to occur, this could be a place where the true five-fold ministry gift evangelist could interact directly with the other Mountains. Evangelists who can share the gospel clearly, in a low-key, business-savvy sort of way, will be needed. In some cases, that role may be filled by an apostle instead. They can sometimes relate better to the leaders as visionaries and know how to share the gospel in a way they will understand and accept. There will probably be a mix of the two. Remember, business is conducted in every Mountain, so there is much potential for these types of meetings.

The gifts of the Spirit were in operation in the FGBMFI meetings. People were healed, received the baptism of the Holy Spirit, and some even received deliverance. The same should be true of these new meetings as they start popping up. Prophets or prophetic people should be included as well to add that ministry dimension, which was not prevalent back in the early days of FGBMFI.

Pastors in the Mountains

The pastor who knows you, personally, may work to encourage you in what you are doing within your Mountain or nudge you to start reaching out and engaging more actively there. That is the indirect influence of training and disciplining you within the Religion Mountain to impact the other Mountains. We will see that this role often functions *within* the other Mountains. Like the other four ministry gifts, the pastor can overlap from the Church in the Religion Mountain to the other Mountains.

There are many who have "pastored" people with whom they worked from the perspective and definition of what that means in the Church. Listening and being interested in people and what they are going through often opens the door to pray with them and opportunities to lead them to the Lord if they do not know Him. If they accept the Lord or are not yet mature in their walk with Him, then the door may be open to work with them to help them mature and grow in the Lord, effectively discipling them as a pastor in a local church would. Of course, this is not limited to people within your workplace. It could be anyone with whom you have regular contact with opportunity to talk – the person who cuts your hair, your masseuse, the person who cleans your house, a caregiver, or your next-door neighbor.

While pastor is mentioned the least in the New Testament, it could be the one to which the most people are called and gifted to fill.

It is interesting that while this five-fold ministry gift is mentioned the least in the New Testament, it could be the one to which the most people are called and gifted to fill. The issue is the Church understanding it correctly and then rightly identifying the people who are called to it. In many local churches today, it is the small group leader who is pastoring (discipling) the people in that group, not "the pastor" of the church. Most of these small group leaders will never hold a theological degree or ministerial credentials, yet they are the ones doing the work of the shepherd for those in their group.

Even with that view, we must keep in mind that as with someone evangelizing versus being an evangelist, the same is true for any of these five ministry gifts. A saint may be "doing the work of the ministry" by serving, exhorting, showing mercy, and giving of themselves, their time, and their money to help someone. That does not mean they are a five-fold ministry gift pastor. The requirement for any five-fold ministry gift is that they are equipping (teaching and training) others. If that person is also teaching and training through discipleship, then they may be a true five-fold pastor even though they are called to operate occupationally in the secular realm.

Final Comments on Five-Fold in the Mountains

Do Your Part

I purposefully delayed delving into Ephesians 4:11-16. It is now time to address it.

> [11] *And He Himself gave some to be apostles, some prophets, some evangelists, and some pastors and teachers,* [12] *for the equipping of the saints for the work of ministry, for the edifying of the body of Christ,* [13] *till we all come to the unity of the faith and of the knowledge of the Son of God, to a perfect man, to the measure of the stature of the fullness of Christ;* [14] *that we should no longer be children, tossed to and fro and carried about with every wind of doctrine, by the trickery of men, in the cunning craftiness of deceitful plotting,* [15] *but, speaking the truth in love, may grow up in all things into Him who is the head – Christ –* [16] *from whom the whole body, joined and knit together by what every joint supplies, according to the effective working by which every part does its share, causes growth of the body for the edifying of itself in love.*

The purpose of what we call the five-fold ministry gifts is not to "do" ministry or to be "ministers." This passage is clear that the reason Christ gave these gifts (in the form of people) to the body was "*for*" – which indicates purpose – "*the equipping of the saints*."

Paul did not stop there. Christ gave us the purpose for which the saints are equipped: "*for the work of ministry*." While we have traditionally called those who go to a Bible College or seminary and become credentialed by an organization "ministers," that is not what makes anyone a minister. *Every* believer (*every* saint) is called to do "*the work of the ministry*." That means *every believer is a minister*. I know that in certain circles we have been acknowledging and saying this for years. Unfortunately, for the most part, we still have not been *acting* like it is true.

Too many parishioners still come to church meetings *to be ministered to* rather than *to minister*. The idea that they might have something to either add to the meeting or to minister to an individual or individuals does not cross their mind. Therefore, it does not cross their mind that they should be looking for opportunities to minister every day, everywhere they go. There are those who say that we should be prepared to minister "9 to 5," implying on our jobs or at school. I say we should be prepared to minister twenty-four hours a day, seven days a week, anytime, anyplace, even when we do not feel like it. Remember Paul's exhortation to Timothy to "Be ready in season and out of season" (2 Timothy 4:2).

Too many parishioners still come to church meetings to be ministered to rather than to minister.

We see that the reason for equipping the saints to be ministers is so that we can all grow up and "*no longer be children, tossed to and fro and carried about with every wind of doctrine*." We need to become grounded in the truth of the Word of God and not get blown off course by everything we hear. We do not want to be like those that Paul warned Timothy about in 2 Timothy 4:3-4. He said, "For the time will come when they will not endure sound doctrine, but … have itching ears … turn their ears away from the truth and [are] turned aside to fables."

It is only when we each grow up and begin to supply our part that "*according to the effective working by which every part does its share,*" the body can grow effectively. *We each have our part to fill.* If we do not fulfill our part, something will be lacking. Our part is not simply ministering among "the brethren" within our local body or even in the Church at large. It is that, but it is more. It is ministering *wherever* we are, *whenever* the opportunity arises – or whenever Holy Spirit prompts us to create the opportunity.

We each have our part to fill. If we do not fill our part, something will be lacking.

When we understand the message of the gospel of Kingdom instead of simply a gospel of salvation, we see that we should always be looking to expand the Kingdom, wherever we are. We need to begin walking in Deuteronomy 11:24, believing "Every place on which the sole of [our] foot treads shall be [ours]." The five-fold ministry gifts should be training us to take our territory – whatever "our territory" may be, in whichever Mountain, we find it, at whatever place in the Mountain we are designed to fill.

Keep Your Wineskin Pliable

I must interject this prophetically. As the Church is being "re-formed," there are things in our doctrine and mindsets that must change to come back into proper alignment with God's plan and His Word. When those truths that were buried by the schemes of the enemy begin to resurface and be taught, many of our brothers and sisters will cry, "Heresy!" They will quote scriptures such as Ephesians 4:14, saying those believing these restored truths are being "tossed to and fro and carried about with every wind of doctrine, by the trickery of men." They will accuse us of having "itching ears" and that we have turned our "ears away from the truth," as Paul warned of in 2 Timothy 4:3-4.

I say this again: *Reformers always pay a price.* If you embrace this reformation, you will end up seeing and understanding certain things differently than you do today. It will not matter if you embrace it as a reformer (forerunner), as an early adopter (one who follows close after), or if you wait until the restored truths become mainstream. To embrace it, there will be beliefs you currently hold that will have to be laid down to accept the truths that God has restored to the Church. Some sacred cows may have to be sacrificed on the altar of truth.

Do not allow your wineskin to become inflexible. Keep soaking it in the water of the Word and allowing the wine of Holy Spirit to flow freely through it.

To successfully make that shift, make sure you are keeping your wineskin soft and pliable by allowing Holy Spirit to constantly flow through you. If you do not, your wineskin will eventually burst, and you will lose the fullness of the Spirit you were still carrying. (See Matthew 9:17.) If you allow your wineskin to burst and lose the flow of the Holy Spirit through you, at that point you are in danger of becoming a persecutor of the new move of God.

Do not allow your wineskin to become inflexible. Keep soaking it in the water of the Word and allowing the wine of Holy Spirit to flow freely through it.

Different Perspective on Five-Fold

I want to briefly address a belief regarding five-fold ministry gifts to which some subscribe. There are those who believe everyone is called to one of the five-fold ministry gifts listed in Ephesians 4:11. Since, percentagewise, there are so few who walk in those offices today, the common response is that most people never realize or fully step into their call.

I do not subscribe to that belief for several reasons. If you do, I doubt I will sway you here. I believe that many who subscribe to that view do so because they see the *characteristics* of one of the five roles in people who are not called to that role within the Church. They do not understand that the *characteristics* of each of these – those with similar personalities and motivational gifts from Romans 12:6-8 – are found in all the Mountains. Everyone has some mix of motivational gifts. Those gifts will manifest in the same or similar ways regardless of the Mountain.

I believe that as more of the Church comes to understand our role as followers of Christ in the other spheres of society, there will be a better understanding of the five-fold ministry gifts within the Church. I also believe that the time and season in which we are now walking will see more true five-fold ministry gifts identified, matured, and functioning within the Church. I believe the saints will begin to operate more powerfully in the gifts given to us by the Holy Spirit (1 Corinthians 12:7-10). With that, I believe we will begin to see signs following *all* of us as they should (Mark 16:17-18).

Chapter 10
Become an Influence

You Have Authority

Just working in a Mountain gives you authority in that Mountain, regardless of your position. It does not matter how insignificant your role may seem; you can still impact the people in the Mountain, which in turn impacts the culture of the Mountain. Remember the story of the young Israelite girl taken captive who became a servant to the wife of Naaman, the commander of the Syrian army. 2 Kings 5:1 tells us that Naaman "was a great and honorable man in the eyes of his master," the king of Syria, and that, "He was also a mighty man of valor, *but* a leper." It was this young captive girl who spoke up about the prophet of the God of Israel who could heal him. Because of her comment to her mistress, Naaman went to the king of Israel, who, of course, could not help him. The prophet heard about it and sent word for Naaman to be sent to him. Elisha then told him to go dip seven times in the Jordan River and he would be healed. He was insulted. After resisting, it was his servants who were with him that convinced him to at least try it and "his flesh was restored like the flesh of a little child, and he was clean" (2 Kings 5:14).

That is not the end of the story. Naaman is not just "made whole" physically; he is changed spiritually as well. Verses 17 and 18 tell us:

> *[17] So Naaman said, "Then, if not, please let your servant be given two mule-loads of earth; for your servant will no longer offer either burnt offering or sacrifice to other gods, but to the Lord. [18] Yet in this thing may the Lord pardon your servant: when my master goes into the temple of Rimmon to worship*

> *there, and he leans on my hand, and I bow down in the temple of Rimmon – when I bow down in the temple of Rimmon, may the Lord please pardon your servant in this thing."*

Elisha granted him both the dirt he requested and permission to serve his master without guilt or condemnation. What is not in this passage, but tradition tells us, is that it was Naaman who brought the message of the God of Israel to Syria. All because an Israeli captive, whose name we do not know, told her mistress about the power of her God and His prophet. Naaman would not have been healed, even after going, if his servants had not convinced him to at least try what the prophet had said to do. We do not know the names of these servants either.

It does not matter how lowly you might feel your position in the Mountain or within the company in which you work is, you can have influence. But only if you speak up when the opportunity presents itself. The young girl dared to speak to her mistress. Naaman's servants dared to speak to him *when he was "in a rage"* (verse 12). It changed his life. No doubt, it changed his wife's life when he returned home. If what has been passed down is true, it changed the lives of an untold number of people. Who knows. What you say might just do that too. But only if you speak up.

> *It does not matter how lowly you might feel your position in the Mountain is, you can have influence.*

In a video series titled "End Times Jesus," Lance Wallnau talks about taking territory for the Kingdom of God within a business. He told how, as a consultant for a Fortune 500 company, he would walk around their corporate offices after others left at the end of the day and pray and claim it for Jesus. As he would discern them, he would command evil spirits operating there to leave. He was not the CEO. He was not even a permanent employee. He was *just* a consultant. But he was being paid by the company and that made him an employee. When he asked God if he had jurisdictional authority to pray as he was for this company, the Lord's response to Him was, "If you are the only Christian in the company, I do not care if you're the janitor. If you've got a job in that company, you're the highest-ranking spiritual authority."[88]

Your position in the company does not matter. What matters is that you know your identity in Christ and your authority as a son or daughter of God. Yet, remember the key Wallnau discovered about finding other like-minded believers and forming a micro church to give the force multiplier needed to deal with the spiritual darkness more effectively.

Where Am I and Where Am I Going?

We must each ask ourselves the following questions:

1. To which Mountain(s) am I called?
2. Where is my place in my Mountain? Am I called with the responsibility of one of the ministry giftings for that Mountain (Apostle/Visionary, Prophet/Strategist, Teacher, Evangelist, Pastor) or to minister (serve, do the work of the ministry) in it elsewhere?
3. Where am I now?
4. Where is God calling me to be?
5. What do I need to do to prepare myself so that I can fulfill what God has called me to do?

Everyone is called to at least one Mountain. God did not place any of us here on earth at this pivotal time to just live a life drifting around without purpose. You have a purpose, a reason for being here, an assignment. If you do not know what that is, it is time to find out. My greatest desire is that when I step from this mortal body into the eternal realm, I hear, “Well done, thy good and faithful servant.” I realized long ago that I could not do something well if I did not know what I was called to do. God does not tell us all of it up front. If He did, it might scare us out of it! Or we might get impatient and produce an Ishmael instead of waiting for the maturing process and the right timing and process to birth Isaac. We must continue to seek Him for revelation of what He purposed for us to be and do before we were conceived. Will you commit to that as I have?

Find out what God has planned and purposed for you and then live that life to its very fullest.

Your role may be as a mother in the Family Mountain who raises godly children that will one day make a significant impact on the Kingdom. That was the primary role for Susanna Wesley, mother of both John and Charles Wesley. She home-schooled all ten of her children and spent individual time with each of them each week. Or you may be called to be an entrepreneur who finances someone else’s vision or project. You might already be running a successful business, or you might have that idea that you have not yet stepped out to try.

Seek God if you do not yet know your place. Keep seeking Him if you do; it might change over time. This applies to questions 3 through 5 above as well. Those are questions we should each ask repeatedly over the course of our lives. Sometimes we may not know where God is calling us to be. In that case, we simply remain obedient to do the things He is leading us to do, *even if that means submitting to things or positions that are neither desirable nor comfortable*. Submit to God’s training process so that you will be prepared for what He knows lies ahead. Your day of convergence will come when it will all make sense.

You may or may not have one of the five-fold ministry giftings in the Religion Mountain or its counterpart in another Mountain. Please realize that having or not having such a call on your life does not make you any more or any less important in the Kingdom. If you do, it makes you more responsible and accountable for what you do and how you use it. "For everyone to whom much is given, from him much will be required," (Luke 12:48). Also, remember Paul's exhortation in Romans 12:6-8. In the New Living Translation (NLT), it reads this way:

> [6] In his grace, God has given us different gifts for doing certain things well. So if God has given you the ability to prophesy, speak out with as much faith as God has given you. [7] If your gift is serving others, serve them well. If you are a teacher, teach well. [8] If your gift is to encourage others, be encouraging. If it is giving, give generously. If God has given you leadership ability, take the responsibility seriously. And if you have a gift for showing kindness to others, do it gladly.

When we stand before the throne to have our lives assessed, we will not be graded on a curve against each other. We will be judged on whether we did what God intended us to do with the talents (gifts and abilities) and opportunities He gave us. Susanna Wesley will be judged on how well she did what God assigned her to do. Her son, Charles, will be judged according to how well he fulfilled the purpose for which he was created. Their roles were vastly different. So is yours. Find out what God has planned and purposed for you and then live that life to its very fullest. Run *your* race well; do not try to run someone else's.

I am reminded of a marksman in the 2004 Olympics who was expected to win the gold medal and, going into his last target, was well ahead of the next competitor. In his exuberance at that moment, when he took aim for his final shot, he got the wrong target in his sights. He hit a perfect bullseye – on the wrong target. There was no doubt he was the best marksman in the competition. He was running his race with excellence. But, at the very end, he got his eyes fixed on someone else's target and lost his prize. Someone else did not take it from him; he lost it. Keep your eyes on *your* prize; do not get distracted by someone else's target.

Final Comments

There are many influencers in each mountain. All do not have to be Christians. What we need are enough that walk in righteousness, act justly, and call good "good" and evil "evil" to re-center public opinion in this nation back on Judeo-Christian values as it once was. We need believers to arise and take the place for which God uniquely created them. Some of those currently in positions who are not operating righteously were created by God to be where they are; they just have not yet surrendered their lives to Him. We must not forget to pray for those who are there as we are working to increase the influence of the righteous in each Mountain. Likewise, do not forget we need candles of light burning all up and down the mountain, not just at the top. Not everyone is called to the top. We need to shine where we are. Isaiah 60:1-3 tells us:

1 Arise, shine;
For your light has come!
And the glory of the Lord is risen upon you.
2 For behold, the darkness shall cover the earth,
And deep darkness the people;
But the Lord will arise over you,
And His glory will be seen upon you.
3 The Gentiles shall come to your light,
And kings to the brightness of your rising.

We need to allow the Lord to arise so that His glory may be seen on us. Then those who do not know Him (the Gentiles) will come to the light shining through us and rulers (those who lead and influence) to the brightness they see around us.

Training those who are either already influencers in a Mountain or have the potential to be a high-level influencer has been discussed. Those positions cannot be held (occupied) unless there are others of like mind letting their righteousness shine all up and down the Mountain.

Only about 2 to 3 percent of Christians work in vocational ministry or for a ministry or para-church organization. Even when we add in others in the Religion Mountain that work for one of the Christian sub-cultures, the vast majority of Christians are still functioning in one of the other six Mountains daily. It is a matter of learning to take our spiritual position and authority there instead of believing the lie of the enemy that we cannot affect change.

As revival is breaking forth around us, we must continue to pray for it to move to awakening. Awakening is where those who have never known God begin to come to Him, often for no apparent reason except the deception that has kept them away suddenly falls off. This, too, is already beginning. Then we must continue to push in prayer and action to bring the reformation needed to all sectors of our society, including the Church.

Reformation has begun in both the Church and in our nation. Therefore, change is coming to both. May we each do our part – that piece for which we were uniquely created and placed on the earth at this time to do. May we see His Kingdom come and His will be done on earth as we work together "As One!"

About the Author

Laurie E. Skipper (BS, MS, MS, ThD) grew up in a Pentecostal church. She was saved at seven, baptized in the Holy Spirit at eight, and has been moving in the gifts of the Holy Spirit corporately and teaching Bible studies since her teens. She parodies Barbara Mandrell saying, "I was Pentecostal when Pentecostal wasn't cool," meaning she was speaking in tongues before it became more widely accepted and practiced during the charismatic renewal.

Laurie's spiritual journey and cross-country moves have taken her back and forth between classical Pentecostal churches and some which had embraced elements of the charismatic renewal. In the early 1980s, she embraced the teachings from the Faith movement. In the mid-1980s, she embraced the teachings and worship coming from the "Third Wave" movement which included teaching on how to flow in the gifts of the Spirit. That set her up to readily embrace further teaching about activation in the gifts of the Spirit encountered in the prophetic movement in the late 1980s. Laurie continued her spiritual journey by embracing the apostolic as it began to emerge in the late 1990s and early 2000s.

As a spiritual trailblazer and pioneer, God has kept Laurie near the forefront of the truths being restored to His Church. However, her standard for embracing any "new" teaching has always been validating it in the Word of God.

Laurie had a successful career, first as a mathematics instructor within the public school system at the secondary and community college levels, transitioning briefly into engineering, and then spending 35+ years in Information Technology (IT). She retired from the corporate realm as a Director in IT. Yet, throughout all of that, Laurie continued to teach the Word and minister prophetically.

Her call as a prophet was recognized by her church leadership in 1990. Since that time, she has not only trained and activated many in moving in the gifts of the Spirit but has also taught and mentored those called into the prophetic, including those called to the office of prophet. While she continues to do both, God is now bringing those teachings and activations into the context of the fuller message of the Kingdom of God and the framework of the message of the Seven Mountain Mandate. Her heart is to see believers activated and demonstrating His gifts everywhere we have influence in our culture.

Academically, she started with degrees in Mathematics Education then returned to graduate school to study Industrial Engineering. Her engineering career quickly morphed into what is now known as Information Technology. It was not until she retired from the IT world that she was finally able to focus on fulfilling a long-time dream and complete her doctorate in theology. Even with that, she continues to study in other areas and says she always will.

Bibliography

Ahn, Ché. *The Reformer's Pledge*. Shippensburg: Destiny Image Publishers, Inc., 2010.

Enlow, Johnny. *Seven Mountain Renaissance: Vision and Strategy through 2050*. New Kensington: Whitaker House, 2015.

Enlow, Johnny. *The Seven Mountain Mantle*. Lake Mary: Creation House, 2009.

Enlow, Johnny. *The Seven Mountain Prophecy*. Lake Mary: Creation House, 2008.

Enlow, Johnny and Elizabeth. *Rainbow God: The Seven Colors of Love*. Unknown: Seven Mountains Publishing, 2013.

Enlow, Johnny and Elizabeth. *RISE: A Reformer's Handbook for the Seven Mountains*. Unknown: Seven Mountain Publishing, 2018.

Hood, Greg. *Kingdom Function of the Five-Fold Ministry and Church Government*. Franklin: Greg Hood Ministries, 2001.

Maiden, Michael. *Turn the World Upside Down: Discipling the Nations with the Seven Mountain Strategy*. Shippensburg: Destiny Image Publishers, Inc., 2011.

Metaxas, Eric. *Amazing Grace: William Wilberforce and the Heroic Campaign to End Slavery*. New York: HarperCollins Publishers, 2007.

Wallnau, Lance, Bill Johnson, Alan Vincent, C. Peter Wagner, Ché Ahn, and Patricia King. *Invading Babylon: The 7 Mountain Mandate*. Shippensburg: Destiny Image Publishers, Inc., 2013.

Recommended Resources

Books

Enlow, Johnny. *Kingdom Come: Understanding the Reign of God on Earth*. Austin: Fedd Books, 2024.

Hood, Greg. *The Gospel of the Kingdom*. Armory: Greg Hood Ministries, 2022.

Munroe, Myles. *Rediscovering the Kingdom, Expanded Edition: Ancient Hope for Our 21st Century World.* Shippensburg: Destiny Image Publishers, Inc., 2010.

Wallnau, Lance. *God's Chaos Candidate: Donald J. Trump and the American Unraveling*. Keller: Killer Sheep Media, Inc., 2016.

Wallnau, Lance, and Mercedes Sparks. *God's Chaos Code: The Shocking Blueprint That Reveals 5 Keys to The Destiny of Nations.* Keller: Killer Sheep Media, Inc., 2020.

Videos

The Seven Mountain Mandate series, listed in sequential order:

Johnny Enlow (@JohnnyElizabethEnlow). "The Seven Mountain Mandate: Overview." YouTube, November 28, 2018. https://www.youtube.com/watch?v=9IbxLOuO5qM.

Johnny Enlow (@JohnnyElizabethEnlow). "The Seven Mountain Mandate: Mountain of Government." YouTube, December 4, 2018. https://www.youtube.com/watch?v=MbVH-wp7nGY.

Johnny Enlow (@JohnnyElizabethEnlow). "The Seven Mountain Mandate: Mountain of Economy." YouTube, December 11, 2018. https://www.youtube.com/watch?v=0scylQEuj2U.

Johnny Enlow (@JohnnyElizabethEnlow). "The Seven Mountain Mandate: Mountain of Education." YouTube, December 18,2018. https://www.youtube.com/watch?v=wi3gmmJdSP4.

Johnny Enlow (@JohnnyElizabethEnlow). "The Seven Mountain Mandate: Mountain of Media." YouTube, January 16, 2019. https://www.youtube.com/watch?v=_NPyZEN3qSQ.

Johnny Enlow (@JohnnyElizabethEnlow). "The Seven Mountain Mandate: Mountain of Family." YouTube, January 29, 2019. https://www.youtube.com/watch?v=P6R3SwWOPWs.

Johnny Enlow (@JohnnyElizabethEnlow). "The Seven Mountain Mandate: Mountain of Religion." YouTube, February 5, 20219. https://www.youtube.com/watch?v=bGuXRQJNWDI.

Johnny Enlow (@JohnnyElizabethEnlow). "The Seven Mountain Mandate: Mountain of Arts & Entertainment." YouTube, February 12, 2019. https://www.youtube.com/watch?v=r2tTbWjPuE4.

Johnny Enlow (@JohnnyElizabethEnlow). "The Seven Mountain Mandate: Extreme World Makeover." YouTube, March 5, 2019. https://www.youtube.com/watch?v=hN10YDefXeU.

Endnotes

Introduction

[1] Paul Petitte, "Revival Sweeping Through College Campuses Impacting Tens of Thousands: 'It's a Movement'," CBN, September 23, 2024, https://cbn.com/news/us/revival-sweeping-through-college-campuses-impacting-tens-thousands-its-movement.

[2] Benjamin Gill, "'Jesus Met Us There': Massive Revival Moment as 10,000 Seek Jesus at University of Arkansas," CBN, September 20, 2024, https://cbn.com/news/us/jesus-met-us-there-massive-revival-moment-10000-seek-jesus-university-arkansas.

[3] Talia Wise, "'They Want God': 8,000 Students Seek Jesus in Huge Kentucky Revival, 2,000 Give Lives to Christ," CBN, February 13, 2025, https://cbn.com/news/us/they-want-god-8000-students-seek-jesus-huge-kentucky-revival-2000-give-lives-christ.

[4] Talia Wise, "5,000 Students Seek Jesus at WVU, Nearly 1,000 Respond to Altar Call: 'Life-Changing Salvation'," CBN, March 12, 2025, https://cbn.com/news/us/5000-students-seek-jesus-wvu-nearly-1000-respond-altar-call-life-changing-salvation.

[5] Michael Foust, "5,000 Students Worship Jesus at UCF: 'God Is Moving in a Powerful Way'," Crosswalk, February 16, 2026,

---

https://www.crosswalk.com/headlines/contributors/michael-foust/5000-students-worship-jesus-at-ucf-god-is-moving-in-a-powerful-way.html.

[6] Benjamin Gill, "America's #2 Party School Gets Hit by Second Wave of Awakening, Hundreds Turn to Christ," CBN, April 02, 2026, https://cbn.com/news/us/americas-2-party-school-gets-hit-second-wave-awakening-hundreds-turn-christ.

[7] Gregory A. Smith, et al., "Decline of Christianity in the U.S. Has Slowed, May Have Leveled Off," Pew Research Center, (February 26, 2025): 7, https://www.pewresearch.org/wp-content/uploads/sites/20/2025/02/PR_2025.02.26_religious-landscape-study_report.pdf.

[8] Stephanie Kramer, et al., "Modeling the Future of Religion in America," Pew Research Center, (September 13, 2022): 7, https://www.pewresearch.org/wp-content/uploads/sites/20/2022/09/US-Religious-Projections_FOR-PRODUCTION-9.13.22.pdf.

Chapter 1

[9] Johnny Enlow, *The Seven Mountain Prophecy*, (Lake Mary: Creation House, 2008), 181.

Chapter 2

[10] Loren Cunningham, "'7 Spheres' Interview of Loren Cunningham on Original Mountains Vision," interviewed by Os Hillman and

---

Kelle Hughes in Atlanta, Georgia, November 19, 2007, transcript, https://7-berge.blogspot.com/2010/07/7-spheres-interview-of-loren-cunningham.html.

[11] Loren Cunningham, "'7 Spheres' Interview of Loren Cunningham on Original Mountains Vision."

[12] Loren Cunningham, "'7 Spheres' Interview of Loren Cunningham on Original Mountains Vision."

[13] Loren Cunningham, "'7 Spheres' Interview of Loren Cunningham on Original Mountains Vision."

[14] Eric Metaxas, *Amazing Grace: William Wilberforce and the Heroic Campaign to End Slavery*, (HarperCollins Publisher, 2007), 68.

[15] Metaxas, *Amazing Grace: William Wilberforce and the Heroic Campaign to End Slavery*, 68.

[16] Metaxas, *Amazing Grace: William Wilberforce and the Heroic Campaign to End Slavery*, 69.

[17] "Abraham Kuyper," Wikipedia, last modified February 21, 2025, 16:07 (UTC), https://en.wikipedia.org/wiki/Abraham_Kuyper.

Chapter 3

[18] Michael Maiden, *Turn the World Upside Down: Discipling the Nations with the Seven Mountain Strategy*, (Shippensburg: Destiny Image Publishers, 2011), 14.

[19] "About Lance Wallnau," Lance Wallnau, accessed April 28, 2025, https://lancewallnau.com/.

---

[20] Lance Wallnau, "2025 Winter Conference Season with Lance Wallnau February 14, 2025, at 7:00 PM" The Family Church at Christian Retreat, Bradenton, FL, February 14, 2025, 1:26:23, https://www.youtube.com/watch?v=hkiZCYXhQZM&t=3582s.

[21] Ché Ahn, *The Reformer's Pledge*, (Shippensburg: Destiny Image Publishers, Inc., 2010), 177-194.

[22] Lance Wallnau, et al, *Invading Babylon: The 7 Mountain Mandate*, (Shippensburg: Destiny Image Publishers, Inc., 2013), 53-73.

[23] "Our Story," Lance Wallnau Ministries, accessed April 25, 2025, https://lancewallnau.com/our-story/.

[24] "Force Multiplier (US DoD Definition)," Military Factory, accessed May 10, 2025, https://www.militaryfactory.com/dictionary/military-terms-defined.php?term_id=2165.

[25] "Force multiplication," Wikipedia, last modified January 16, 2025, https://en.wikipedia.org/wiki/Force_multiplication.

Chapter 4

[26] "Meet the Enlows," Restore7, accessed April 28, 2025, https://restore7.org/johnny-elizabeth.

[27] Johnny and Elizabeth Enlow, "Big God – Part 1" Documentary, Restore7 TV, May 18, 2024, 28:30, https://watch.restore7.tv/player/51902/650921.

---

[28] Johnny and Elizabeth Enlow, "Big God – Part 1" Documentary, 1:38:12

[29] Johnny and Elizabeth Enlow, "Big God – Part 2" Documentary, Restore7 TV, Franklin, TN, May 25, 2024, 16:50, https://watch.restore7.tv/player/51902/652189.

[30] Johnny and Elizabeth Enlow, "Big God – Part 2" Documentary, 17:48.

[31] Johnny and Elizabeth Enlow, "Big God – Part 2" Documentary, 14:18.

[32] Johnny and Elizabeth Enlow, "Big God – Part 2" Documentary, 15:12.

[33] Johnny and Elizabeth Enlow, "Big God – Part 2" Documentary, 25:50.

[34] Johnny and Elizabeth Enlow, "Big God – Part 2" Documentary, 26:46.

[35] Johnny and Elizabeth Enlow, "Big God – Part 2" Documentary, 29:20.

[36] Johnny and Elizabeth Enlow, "Big God – Part 2" Documentary, 31:08.

[37] Johnny and Elizabeth Enlow, "Big God – Part 3" Documentary, Restore7 TV, Franklin, TN, June 1, 34:59, https://watch.restore7.tv/player/51902/653392.

[38] Johnny and Elizabeth Enlow, "Big God – Part 3" Documentary, 30:24.

[39] Johnny and Elizabeth Enlow, "Big God – Part 3" Documentary, 26:01.

---

[40] Johnny and Elizabeth Enlow, “Big God – Part 3” Documentary, 26:43.

[41] Johnny and Elizabeth Enlow, “Big God – Part 3” Documentary, 29:09.

[42] Johnny and Elizabeth Enlow, “Big God – Part 3” Documentary, 29:22.

[43] Johnny and Elizabeth Enlow, “Big God – Part 2” Documentary, 49:23.

[44] Johnny and Elizabeth Enlow, “Big God – Part 2” Documentary, 58:16.

[45] Johnny and Elizabeth Enlow, “Big God – Part 2” Documentary, 1:02:21.

[46] Johnny and Elizabeth Enlow, “Big God – Part 3” Documentary, 31:22.

[47] Johnny and Elizabeth Enlow, *RISE: A Reformer's Handbook for the Seven Mountains*, (Unknown: Seven Mountain Publishing, 2018), 31-127.

Chapter 5

[48] Johnny Enlow, *The Seven Mountain Prophecy*, 47-179.

[49] Johnny and Elizabeth Enlow, *Rainbow God: The Seven Colors of Love*, (Unknown: Seven Mountains Publishing, 2013), 49-212.

[50] Johnny and Elizabeth Enlow, *RISE: A Reformer's Handbook for the Seven Mountains*, 31-127.

[51] Michael Maiden, *Turn the World Upside Down: Discipling the Nations with the Seven Mountain Strategy*, 59-150.

---

[52] Matthew Lysiak, "Media in Meltdown," Newsmax, May 2025, 55.

[53] Lance Wallnau, "Endgame: A Time for Peace and A Time for War, Part 2 of 2" Teaching Series on CD 2, 2019, 5:27, https://lance-learning.myshopify.com/collections/7mountains/products/endgame-a-time-for-peace-and-a-time-for-war.

[54] "Fairness Doctrine," Britannica.com, accessed April 25, 2025, https://www.britannica.com/topic/Fairness-Doctrine.

[55] Britannica.com, "Fairness Doctrine."

[56] Johnny and Elizabeth Enlow, *RISE: A Reformer's Handbook for the Seven Mountains*, 33.

[57] Johnny Enlow, *The Seven Mountain Prophecy*, 58.

[58] Lance Wallnau, "Endgame: A Time for Peace and A Time for War, Part 2 of 2," 1:22.

[59] Johnny and Elizabeth Enlow, *RISE: A Reformer's Handbook for the Seven Mountains*, 47.

[60] Johnny and Elizabeth Enlow, *RISE: A Reformer's Handbook for the Seven Mountains*, 75.

[61] Lance Wallnau, "Endgame: A Time for Peace and A Time for War, Part 2 of 2," 3:30.

[62] Lance Wallnau, "Endgame: A Time for Peace and A Time for War, Part 2 of 2," 3:09.

[63] Lance Wallnau, "Endgame: A Time for Peace and A Time for War, Part 2 of 2," 1:39.

[64] Binge Now (@BingeNow), "Most Shocking Hallmark Actors Who Left the Network," YouTube video, May 18, 2025, 00:01-12:37, https://www.youtube.com/watch?v=Nauj3HajvsI.

[65] "Economy," Merrian-Webster Unabridged Dictionary, Merriam-Webster, accessed April 12, 2025, https://unabridged.merriam-webster.com/unabridged/economy.

[66] "Economic," Merrian-Webster Unabridged Dictionary, Merriam-Webster, accessed April 12, 2025, https://unabridged.merriam-webster.com/unabridged/economic.

[67] Michael Maiden, *Turn the World Upside Down: Discipling the Nations with the Seven Mountain Strategy*, 72.

[68] "Sharia Law In America: Sharia Law Advancing in America," BillionBibles.org, accessed April 13, 2025, https://www.billionbibles.org/sharia/america-sharia-law.html.

[69] "Spread of Islam," BillionBibles.org, accessed April 13, 2025, https://www.billionbibles.org/sharia/islam-expansion.html.

[70] Rod D. Martin (@roddmartin), "May Day," Substack, May 1, 2025, https://www.rodmartin.org/p/may-day-629.

[71] "Luke 16," Bible Study Tools, Bible Versions - NAS, accessed May 4, 2025, https://www.biblestudytools.com/nas/luke/16.html.

[72] "Shrewd," Bible Study Tools, New Testament Greek Lexicon - NAS accessed May 4, 2025,

---

https://www.biblestudytools.com/lexicons/greek/nas/phronimos.htm l.

[73] "Occupy," Merrian-Webster Unabridged Dictionary, Merriam-Webster, accessed April 12, 2025, https://unabridged.merriam webster.com/unabridged/occupy.

[74] Michael Maiden, *Turn the World Upside Down: Discipling the Nations with the Seven Mountain Strategy*, 141.

[75] Michael Maiden, *Turn the World Upside Down: Discipling the Nations with the Seven Mountain Strategy*, 106.

Chapter 6

[76] Johnny and Elizabeth Enlow, *RISE: A Reformer's Handbook for the Seven Mountains*, 31-127.

Chapter 7

[77] Johnny and Elizabeth Enlow, *RISE: A Reformer's Handbook for the Seven Mountains*, 31-127.

[78] "Ephesians 4," Bible Study Tools, Bible Versions - NAS, accessed April 17, 2025, https://www.biblestudytools.com/nas/ephesians/4.html.

[79] "Poimen," Bible Study Tools, New Testament Greek Lexicon - NAS accessed April 17, 2025, https://www.biblestudytools.com/lexicons/greek/nas/poimen.html.

---

[80] "1 Corinthians 12," Bible Study Tools, Bible Versions - NAS, accessed April 17, 2025, https://www.biblestudytools.com/nas/1-corinthians/12.html.

[81] "Protos, Bible Study Tools," New Testament Greek Lexicon - NAS accessed April 17, 2025, https://www.biblestudytools.com/lexicons/greek/nas/protos.html.

[82] "Deuteros," Bible Study Tools, New Testament Greek Lexicon - NAS accessed April 17, 2025, https://www.biblestudytools.com/lexicons/greek/nas/deuteros.html.

[83] "Tritos," Bible Study Tools, New Testament Greek Lexicon - NAS accessed April 17, 2025, https://www.biblestudytools.com/lexicons/greek/nas/tritos.html.

Chapter 8

[84] Johnny and Elizabeth Enlow, *RISE: A Reformer's Handbook for the Seven Mountains*, 33.

Chapter 9

[85] Lance Wallnau (@LanceWallnauShow), "Supernatural Business Strategy – won't look like church," YouTube video, May 9, 2025, 20:07, https://www.youtube.com/live/sRx2nw2xf-Y?si=i6miLC3w86cCZwCD.

---

[86] "2024 Year End," Restore Seven, accessed April 18, 2025, https://restore7.org/2024-year-end/.

[87] Lance Wallnau (@LanceWallnauShow), "Supernatural Business Strategy – won't look like church," 13:07.

Chapter 10

[88] Lance Wallnau, "End Times Jesus, Part 2" Lord of Hosts Church, Omaha, NE, December 6, 2023, 25:57, https://lance-learning.myshopify.com/collections/frontpage/products/end-times-jesus.

www.ingramcontent.com/pod-product-compliance
Lightning Source LLC
LaVergne TN
LVHW010917110826
845149LV00013B/2396